04/17

GREATEST
WALKS OF
THE WORLD

IN ASSOCIATION WITH
TIMPSON

Also available

The 50 Greatest Rugby Union Players of All Time

The 50 Most Influential Britons of the Last 100 Years

The 50 Greatest Train Journeys of the World

Geoff Hurst's Greats: England's 1966 Hero Selects His
Finest Ever Footballers

David Gower's Greatest Half-Century

the
50

GREATEST
WALKS OF
THE WORLD

BARRY STONE

Published in the UK in 2016 by
Icon Books Ltd, Omnibus Business Centre,
39–41 North Road, London N7 9DP
email: info@iconbooks.com
www.iconbooks.com

Sold in the UK, Europe and Asia
by Faber & Faber Ltd, Bloomsbury House,
74–77 Great Russell Street,
London WC1B 3DA or their agents

Distributed in the UK, Europe and Asia
by TBS Ltd, TBS Distribution Centre, Colchester Road,
Frating Green, Colchester CO7 7DW

Distributed in Australia and New Zealand
by Allen & Unwin Pty Ltd,
PO Box 8500, 83 Alexander Street,
Crows Nest, NSW 2065

Distributed in South Africa by
Jonathan Ball, Office B4, The District,
41 Sir Lowry Road, Woodstock 7925

Distributed in India by Penguin Books India,
7th Floor, Infinity Tower – C, DLF Cyber City,
Gurgaon 122002, Haryana

Distributed in Canada by Publishers Group Canada,
76 Stafford Street, Unit 300,
Toronto, Ontario M6J 2S1

Distributed in the USA
by Publishers Group West,
1700 Fourth Street, Berkeley, CA 94710

ISBN: 978-178578-063-9
Book People edition ISBN: 978-178578-087-5

Images – see individual pictures

Typeset and designed by Simmons Pugh

Printed and bound in the UK by Clays Ltd, St Ives plc

CONTENTS

ABOUT THE AUTHOR

B arry Stone began his writing career in 1998 as a travel writer before authoring his first book in 2007, *I Want to be Alone*, on the history of hermits and recluses. Nine more titles have followed, and in between books he indulges his passion for walking and taking to trails wherever in the world he finds himself when wearing his travel writer's hat. Barry lives on a quiet acre in Picton, an hour's drive south of Sydney with his wife Yvonne and children Jackson and Truman. He rarely has a day when he is neither writing nor walking.

INTRODUCTION

Walking, if you want to reduce it to its base mechanics, is little more than a 'controlled fall', a forward movement initiated by the legs, one of which balances us in an upright position before pushing us forward, while the other swings through in a rhythmic motion just in time to prevent us from collapsing flat on our faces. If you believe the best guess of evolutionary biologists it's likely the advent of walking – of becoming bipedal – arose 4–5 million years ago when our ancestors first became providers for family units and so needed to free up their 'hands' in order to bring home food and provisions. At the same time that our heels, hips and knees were becoming enlarged to carry the extra weight required of them, walking on two legs began to free up those same hands for rock-throwing in order both to procure food and prevent the throwers from becoming food themselves. Over time – a *lot* of time – what began as something that was purposeful and survival-driven, a process of natural selection, morphed to become our most efficient mode of travel. From an exo-skeletal point of view running is, by contrast, 75 per cent *less efficient* than walking. Which I guess means apologies are in order to all the joggers out there who think it better to run than walk. Millions of years of trial and error, and the science of human design, say otherwise.

The era of 'recreational walking' – walking for pleasure – was inaugurated in England in the late 18th and early 19th centuries partly as a reaction against increasing industrialisation, partly because the 'Industrial Revolution' brought increased leisure time to an already leisurely aristocracy, and partly nudged along by the Age of Enlightenment. But mostly it was thanks to the era of heroic Romanticism, which lauded the visceral emotive responses born from getting out and confronting the raw beauty of nature, the expressions of which were then being seen everywhere in art, music and literature. 'Pedestrianism' – the pastime of watching other people simply walking – became for a time the largest spectator sport in late 19th century America, eclipsing even baseball, which was still in the process of finding its own 'legs'. Walking marathons were so popular they began to take on gladiatorial dimensions when they were extended over so many days they doubled as rather gruesome endurance tests in how not to sleep. How different that is to the 'new pedestrianism' of today advocated by the American urban designer and futurist Michael Arth – redesigning urban spaces where walking and cycle paths take the place of roads, pushing the bitumen and those horrid cars that go with them out to a town's perimeter, thus returning cities to the people.

People who indulge in recreational walking in the 21st century do so for many reasons. Me? Well, the reason I walk is not because I like the physical act of walking so much as because I like the landscapes, gorges, ridgelines and suspension bridges through and over which it takes me. I walk because for me it is reductive – it simplifies life, reduces it to a few core decisions. Turn left. Turn right. Go straight. Keep going. Ignore the weather. Be inventive. Don't look back. I like to walk because it is a slow pursuit, rhythmic and repetitive and purposeful and exhilarating. My feet have taken me to places no other mode of transport could: through the sinewy web of iron and steel that makes up the 52,800 tonnes of the Sydney Harbour Bridge, thankfully now accessible to all who want to climb it and a prime example of how our urban environments are becoming increasingly accessible with every new piece of adapted infrastructure; and along the High Line, an old elevated rail line through New York's meatpacking district, now a triumph of urban renewal *National Geographic* called the 'Miracle above Manhattan'. Whether negotiating the fractured limestone pavements of Ireland's Burren Way, rock scrambling through Utah's Buckskin Gulch, moving over ice floes in the Russian arctic or along the Cornish coast – my mind works best when these places slow it down, when everything you need for the day is on your back and when the promise of a well-grassed campsite, cosy hotel, or B&B is all you need to keep you moving forward.

When walking I can be the vagabond 'of no fixed address' I've always longed to be, a wanderer who seeks anonymity and passes through landscapes unnoticed, a passive participant in life. I walk because, in words echoed by the French philosopher Frederic Gros, I have 'a need for contemplation'. Contemplative walking is what inspired Walt Whitman, Robert Frost, William Wordsworth and C. S. Lewis. It frees up the mind to find rhythms otherwise suppressed by the demands of everyday life. It problem solves and 'leaves behind', according to Jean-Jacques Rousseau, 'all base and terrestrial sentiments'. Rousseau's mind only worked, he said, when his legs were in motion. Walking may not of itself provide solutions to life's complexities, but it can facilitate them, expose them. Whittle them down into manageable, bite-sized chunks.

There have been times when I've been so immersed in the distractions and random thoughts I've conjured up that I've failed to negotiate the next step. I've had my fair share of walking mishaps. 'Would you like me to carry you?' my guide asked when he saw me struggling down a stepped section of trail on the Kali Ghandaki gorge, the ligaments in my right knee well and truly stretched thanks to a single ill-timed step. Pride, of course, prevented me from accepting his offer. On

Italy's Alta Via 1, I slid 30 metres down a snow slope after missing a foot hole while daydreaming, and cannoned into the only protruding rock there was – a fortunate trajectory, it turned out, as it prevented me continuing down the hill a further 100 metres. I've rolled down a slope above a Norwegian fjord, grasping at tussocks of grass to help slow my descent. I've even fallen off a suspension bridge.

The 50 walks in this book represent a cross-section of mountain and cross-country trails, circular loops, and historic and coastal walks that showcase the enviable network of trails that criss-cross the United Kingdom but also include some of the world's classic trails such as the Appalachian Trail and the Tour du Mont Blanc. There are trails here that we should all be a little more familiar with than we are, such as Ireland's Dingle Way and the awe-inspiring Trotternish Ridge on the Isle of Skye, as well as many of the ones we 'think' we know – the Pennine Way, the Coast to Coast, and the Cotswold Way.

We live in a modern world in which we are increasingly being 'moved' rather than moving , helped along to wherever it is we want to go by planes, trains, automobiles, electric bicycles, escalators, travelators, segways and hoverboards. Our comforts and conveniences are sapping our strength, and this is no recent phenomenon. Studies at Cambridge University suggest that ever since we gravitated from hunter-gatherers to farmers, our mobility and lower limb strength have been on a gradual decline. Humans, put simply, are past their peak. And urbanisation and a more sedentary lifestyle are to blame.

Now that's not to say that getting out and going for a walk – even a lifetime of very long walks – is going to reverse the effects of the last few thousand post-hunter-gatherer years.

But it's a start.

THE 50 GREATEST WALKS
OF THE WORLD

---

50. WHITE HORSE TRAIL
Wiltshire, England

Distance: 144 km
Grade: Easy
Time: 8–9 days

They are scattered right across Great Britain – 57 figures (gigantotomy) and horses (leucippotomy) carved into chalk and limestone hills in areas where their exposed 'whiteness' contrasts well with darker soil or grassy surrounds. There were once many more. Most were created over the last three or four hundred years, not as ancient as their graceful Celtic-like forms might suggest, although Oxfordshire's Uffington White Horse, a masterpiece of minimalist art, dates to the Iron Age or late Bronze Age and was itself the inspiration for other white horse carvings – including the eight examples you can now see as you make your way along Wiltshire's White Horse Trail.

When it comes to white horses, Wiltshire is without doubt the 'county of counties'. Its oldest and largest, set on the site of an even more ancient carving which it completely covers, is Westbury White Horse, cut in 1778 on the boundary of Bratton Downs above the Vale of Pewsey. Westbury White Horse was restored in 1853 and again in 1872, and in 1873 a line of edging stones was added to help keep the chalk in place. Pewsey White Horse, cut on Pewsey Hill in 1937 close to an earlier example dating from the late 1700s which scholars think may have included a rider, was designed

Photo: Mcbish

and cut to honour the coronation of George VI. The Alton Barnes White Horse on Milk Hill appeared in 1812, and in 1804 students at a school in Preshute designed the 'tiny' (19 m nose to tail) Preshute, or Marlborough, White Horse. The Winterbourne Bassett White Horse was likely cut in 1838 by Henry Eatwell, the Parish Clerk of Broad Hinton, most likely to commemorate the coronation of Queen Victoria. Broad Town White Horse, visible from the village of Broad Town, probably dates to 1863/64 when it was cut by a local farmer, William Simmonds, or could be older if the claims of a curator at the Imperial War Museum that he scoured it with a friend in 1813 are to be believed. Cherhill White Horse, Wiltshire's second oldest (1780) and second largest (43 m ear to hoof), sits below the Iron Age ruins of Oldbury Castle. The county's youngest figure, the Devizes White Horse just north of the town of Devizes on Roundway Hill, cut in 1999 to usher in the new millennium, was based on the design of the now barely visible Snob's White Horse (1845), a figure that has defied several attempts to have it re-cut and is therefore not counted in the list of horses the trail aids you in discovering.

The White Horse Trail takes you to each horse in turn through the lovely rolling hills of central Wiltshire's chalk downs, and while you are certainly welcome to walk the trail in its entirety, each horse has its own approach trail so it is possible to pick and choose which particular horses you'd most like to see. Driving to each horse and walking the trails to their individual viewing points is of course an option, but for those who have a week or more to spare and plan to walk the trail in its entirety, a good starting point is the car park above the Westbury White Horse that skirts a firing range on Salisbury Plain. From Westbury, metalled roads, bridleways, farm tracks, bogs, sleeper bridges and rutted tracks can then get you the 38 km or so via Redhorn Hill to Pewsey, but Westbury's remoteness from the remaining white horses makes this the one section you're probably going to want to drive.

The 18 km from Pewsey White Horse to Marlborough White Horse outside Preshute begins with a lovely walk through uncultivated fields into Pewsey and briefly along the Kennet and Avon Canal towpath. From there continue on to the Mid-Wilts Way (MWW), a lovely rural walk in its own right that runs for 109 km from Ham near Inkpen to Mere, not far from Warminster. Join the Wansdyke Path (more on this wonderful path shortly) on the edge of West Woods, pass through Short Oak Copse and make for Preshute House in Marlborough College, where the Marlborough White Horse can be seen behind the college's tennis courts, sitting in its shallow slope on Granham Hill.

Just 10 km away is Winterbourne Bassett White Horse, reached via Totterdown Wood and along the Ridgeway, long considered Britain's oldest road. The 10-km trail to Broad Town and the Broad Town White Horse begins on the Ridgeway, takes a route through the grounds of Bincknoll Castle and neighbouring Bincknoll Wood, and ends with a trail through brambles, thistles and nettles that may or may not be open to the public thanks to landslips and the path being overgrown, though the alternative approach via Horns Lane and Chapel Lane into Broad Town is easy enough.

The 12.5 km to Cherhill White Horse starts with the crossing of a succession of fields and farm gates until you reach the hamlets of Clevancy and Highway, beyond which you'll have your first sighting of Cherhill's Lansdowne Monument, a 38-m-high obelisk erected by the 3rd Marquis of Lansdowne to commemorate his ancestor William Petty – scientist, philosopher, and charter member of the Royal Society. The Cherhill White Horse is a ten-minute walk from the monument on the hillside below, on a slope so steep that after it was cut children from Cherhill would slide down the figure on sacks and trays. A major renovation was conducted in 2002 which involved re-cutting the horse's outline and resurfacing it with more than 160 tons of fresh chalk.

From Cherhill it is 15 km to Alton Barnes White Horse, an historic treasure-trove of a walk that has you briefly treading an old Roman road before joining up again with the Wansdyke Path, which here follows as best it can a long ditch and embankment dating to the Dark Ages (400 to 700 CE). Constructed by persons unknown on an east-west alignment, the Wansdyke ditch is one of the UK's largest (and least-known) linear earthworks.

Passing more farm tracks, kissing gates and barns you leave the Wansdyke Path and enter Pewsey Downs Nature Reserve, famous not only for the Alton Barnes White Horse which now lies before you on Milk Hill, but also as a Special Area of Conservation in what is a classic chalk down habitat with its early gentians and an orchid-rich grassland that includes a proliferation of burnt-tip and frog orchids that help support the reserve's impressive butterfly population. The Alton Barnes White Horse underwent a significant restoration in 2010 when 150 tons of fresh chalk was helicoptered to the site where volunteers then got to work on giving the figure a much-needed facelift.

The 19-km walk to Devizes starts with a visit to Adam's Grave, a Neolithic long barrow on the summit of Walker's Hill that was opened in 1860 by ethnologist and archaeologist John Thurnam who found several incomplete skeletons and a leaf-shaped spearhead inside. A delightful 11-km walk along the Kennet and Avon Canal towpath through the villages of All Cannings and Horton leads to the gorgeous tree-lined avenue of Quakers Walk before a series of hedges, tarmac roads and a wooden kissing gate brings you to the Devizes Millennium White Horse. Designed in 1999 by a former pupil of Devizes Grammar School, Peter Greed, and the only white horse in Wiltshire to face to the right, it was executed by more than 200 enthusiastic locals and now forms the logo of the Devizes Nursteed Primary School.

Sadly, not all of Wiltshire's white horses have survived. The Rockley White Horse, discovered on Rockley Down in 1948 when the ground above it was ploughed, was lost when the chalk was dispersed, while a horse at Ham Hill cut in the 1860s was lost long ago as it was just an excavated shape with no chalk infill.

The White Horse Trail is an undemanding, gentle walk through a peaceful part of southern England that is filled with history and mysticism. It gets you close to prehistoric Avebury and Silbury Hill, part of the Stonehenge, Avebury and Associated Sites UNESCO World Heritage Site, and includes tantalising glimpses on to some fabulous trails including the Wansdyke, the Ridgeway, and sections of the Kennet and Avon Canal towpath.

49. MONMOUTHSHIRE AND BRECON CANALS
Monmouthshire / Powys, Wales

Distance: 51.5 km
Grade: Easy
Time: 2–3 days

It's a mouthful, isn't it, having to say Monmouthshire and Brecon canals all the time, which is why those who work on

Photo: Greg Willis

it every day prefer to call it, simply, the 'Mon and Brec'. But it wasn't always the single waterway it is today. It began its life as two canals: the Monmouthshire Canal, authorised by an Act of Parliament in 1792 with its main line from Newport to Pontnewynydd (20 km long, 42 locks, rising 136.3 m) opening in 1796 and its Crumlin Arm (18 km, 32 locks, rising 109 m) following in 1799. The other canal, the Brecknock and Abergavenny Canal, was opened in stages from 1797 to 1799 and was originally meant to join with the River Usk near Caerleon but instead was linked to the Monmouthshire Canal at Pontypool.

The canals, built by Navigators (Navvies) to transport iron, coal, stone and processed lime, began declining in profitability in the mid-1800s with the arrival of the railways, and sections routinely began to be abandoned. Commercial traffic ceased in 1933, and in 1962 they closed altogether. Restoration work to convert the canals to recreational waterways, however, soon commenced under the auspices of the newly formed British Waterways, with work on Brynich Lock near Brecon in 1968. After suffering all of the usual ravages associated with more than a century of decline, the canal reopened from Pontypool to Brecon in 1970. It has since evolved into one of the most spectacular and scenic canals to be found anywhere in Great Britain.

Walking (or mountain biking) its towpath, almost all of which passes through Brecon Beacons National Park, is a delight as it winds its way from Brecon to Pontypool past farmlands and woodlands, hugging mountain slopes above the valley of the River Usk. Not being connected to the broader network of British canals means there is far less boat traffic on its slow waters which makes for a quieter, more intimate experience than one generally has on a British canal. The wildlife here is particularly impressive too, with the valley's blanket of wildflowers and the canal being a magnet for birds such as kingfishers, herons, moorhens, swans and mallards. There are also several additional trails you can pick up along the way, like the Henry Vaughan Walk, named in honour of the well-known 17th-century poet that begins in the village of Talybont-on-Usk.

The walk proper, however, begins in Brecon and from Brecon Basin it's about 4 km to the first lock at Brynich and from there to the five locks at Llangynidr – these come as something of a surprise on this canal which is a contour canal, meaning banks of locks are a rarity. The next 37 km to Pontymoile are lock-free – an impressive accomplishment in itself considering the contours of the hills – and often wind under gorgeous canopies of overhanging trees and pass through towns such as Pencelli, Talybont with its above-mentioned Henry Vaughan Walk and Crickhowell, with its Iron Age and Norman remains as well as the spectacular arched bridge over the River Usk, built in 1706 and added to in 1828–30 with thirteen arches on its upstream side, yet only twelve on its downstream!

Gilwern, once a hub of 19th-century industry, is next, with its old tramroads leading to 19th-century limestone quarries and yet more trail diversions, this time taking us to the open moorlands of Llangattock mountain, an undulating plateau that rises to a height of 530 m and formed from coarse sandstones and pockmarked by shakeholes – sinkholes caused by percolating groundwater.

On a canal with a wealth of historic sites, one that should not be missed is Goytre Wharf with its wonderfully preserved lime kilns. At the time of the restoration of the canal in the 1960s Goytre Wharf existed only as a moorage for a few local boats and a boat hire company. It still has its moorage basin, but now the range of vessels is far more eclectic since undergoing its own detailed restoration in 2000.

Walking the canal is more a stroll than a walk. Its industrial history slows you down, but so do its more basic diversions. There is the Royal Oak Pub in Pencelli, the Tipple 'n' Tiffin cafe at Brecon's Theatr Brycheiniog, The White Hart Inn and The Star Inn in Talybont, and the lovely cafe and restaurant at Goytre Wharf. The waterway that was once an industrial corridor bringing raw materials from surrounding quarries along horse-drawn tramroads, incorporating aqueducts over Brynich and Gilwern and the 343-m Ashford Tunnel, is now a canal system built for walking, cycling, canoeing and boating, a delightful reinvention of one of Britain's most isolated – and idyllic – canal systems.

48. LLANGOLLEN ROUND
Denbighshire, Wales

Distance: 53 km
Grade: Easy to Moderate
Time: 2–4 days

They call it the 'Permanent Challenge' – to conquer in a single day the summits surrounding the beautiful Vale of Llangollen on the fully waymarked, high-level 53-km Llangollen Round on the Welsh borders. All you have to do is rise early, have breakfast, and make your way to the Tyn Dwr Outdoor Centre where there will be someone to stamp your route card, give you your Permanent Challenge pack, and take a note of your time. Then off you go, either clockwise or anti-clockwise until you reach the half-way point at the Ponderosa Cafe on Horseshoe Pass, where you collect your next stamp. Then it's a walk/dash to the finish line back at Tyn Dwr where your time is again noted and you receive your personalised certificate that shows your time and the distance covered. And no matter how exhausted you feel at the end of all this you'll be glad you did it, because you've just completed in a day what most people take three or four to do. Plus your fee of six pounds for the privilege of doing it in a day will be going to Cancer Research UK, the Llangollen branch of which was responsible for devising the route.

Of course there's nothing to prevent you from making a contribution to CRUK and then doing it in four days anyway, and plenty of reasons why you should not, the least of which is the lovely mix of limestone grasslands, open heather moorlands, and woodlands both deciduous and coniferous that makes walking here such a delight and something to linger over. And for those who are navigationally challenged the trail is a peach – your starting point of Llangollen is almost always visible as you circle it in the hills above.

Most who take the four-day option begin in Llangollen, the attractive market town on the River Dee famous for its annual Eisteddfod and for Chirk Castle, constructed between 1295 and 1310 to keep the Welsh under English rule. The River Dee is crossed twice on the trail: once via the lovely 1660 Carrog Bridge in Carrog, the last stop on the popular Llangollen Steam Railway line; and once courtesy of the magnificent Pontcysyllte Aqueduct, the 307-m-long 'stream in the sky'. Completed in 1805 using local stone, and a World Heritage Site since 2009, Pontcysyllte is Britain's longest and highest (38 m) aqueduct with eighteen piers, nineteen arches, and is fed by the waters of nearby Horseshoe Falls. While it is a part of the official trail, there

Photo: Roger W Haworth

is also a ground-hugging alternative for those who would prefer not to cross it.

The views along the trail are not to be trifled with – Snowdon and the mountain vistas of northern Wales, the Mersey estuary, the Cheshire Plain, the limestone escarpment of Wenlock Edge with its well-preserved woodlands tumbling down its steep slopes, the Shropshire Hills, and of course the Dee Valley. There's even an Iron Age fort on Llantysilio Mountain (Moel y Gaer – Welsh for 'Bald Hill of the Fortress'), with its single rampart and segmented ditch.

The trail is divided into six segments of varying lengths, determined by their proximity to road and rail connections. Unless you intend pitching a tent it's best to walk a segment and return to Llangollen that evening, before setting out on the next segment the following day. There is a regular bus service out of Llangollen to points on the trail. Ascents and descents are generally fairly gentle, the exception being an 11.4-km stretch that takes in several summits in quick succession over a variety of terrain, including a brief walk over shingles, though no scrambling is required.

Once back in Llangollen if you still have some walking left in you, you can tackle the Llangollen History Trail, a 9.5-km walk that begins in town on Castle Street and takes you to the Llangollen Canal, opened in 1805 to carry slate from surrounding quarries to England's burgeoning cities. A 3-km walk on its towpath goes to Horseshoe Falls, a semi-circular weir designed by Thomas Telford to divert water to the nearby Shropshire Union Canal. The trail also includes Llantysilio church, originally a 13th-century chapel that was enlarged in 1869, the ruins of Valle Crucis Abbey, founded by Cistercian monks in 1201 and once Wales's richest abbey after Tintern, and finally the picturesque ruins of Dinas

Bran Castle, abandoned in 1282. Which amounts to a lot of history, both built and natural, for one very small valley.

47. KEENAGH LOOP WALK
County Mayo, Ireland

Distance: 12 km
Grade: Moderate
Time: 4 hours

This lovely loop in Ireland's County Mayo packs a lot into what is a fairly compact trail – panoramic mountain views, clear-running streams and rivers, and a beautiful valley – all set in a wilderness of ethereal blanket bogs, Ireland's most celebrated type of peatland with a peat substrate that can range in depth from 2 to 7 m underneath a grassy surface of pools, flushes and swallow holes. Here you are in the midst of what could be called Ireland's 'blanket bog coast', a world of low-lying coastal plains which extend through Donegal and Galway – rich wetlands that contain more than 90 per cent water and are in fact vast water reservoirs that support a rich degree of biodiversity including plants, birds, invertebrates and mosses. There are even prehistoric farming landscapes and artefacts hidden beneath in its peat-filled depths. No wonder, then, that those who know better become upset when areas like this are unfairly maligned and referred to as 'wastelands'.

The Keenagh Loop Walk begins at Bellanaderg Bridge, 20 km outside the town of Castlebar, and crosses the Boghadoon River where you follow an old road towards Newport

Photo: Ben Brookshank

before branching off at a three-way junction and through Derreen. Next, head south/southwest on a broad, grass-covered track that takes you up over the eastern shoulder of Letterkeeghaun. Continue on the grassy trail for 3 km past a concrete water tower and the edge of a forest where the trail then bears to the right and takes you over a large expanse of typically boggy ground until you reach a small river. There are waterfalls to admire here as you follow a river for 1 km or so towards the remote and spectacular Glendorragha Valley. As you make your way through the valley keep on the lookout for a line of old timber fence posts, and when you reach them turn right and prepare yourself for a little bit of climbing as you ascend along a small tributary of the river you've been tracing for a 1-km-long slog up to a mountain pass below Knockaffertag, although the climb is a gentle one. After conquering the pass you then descend via an old sheep track on a north/northwest line down past some abandoned farmhouses to a small farm track and on to a small road which takes you back to your starting point.

Walking the Keenagh Loop is an overwhelmingly peaceful, serene experience. This is a genuine wilderness, with what seems like an ocean of grass around you, while peaks like Croagh Patrick far off on the horizon present a haunting vista which only adds to the sense of isolation, not to mention the invigorating sight of Nephin, the conical shaped mountain of quartzite that has been revered – and climbed – for generations. The second-highest mountain in Connaught, Nephin is a wonderful climb, with a route to the summit of some 10 km over hillocky, heather-clad slopes.

The rivers and streams you pass on the Keenagh Loop, if the wind isn't blowing, supply pretty much the only noise that is not being made by you, and the feeling you get being here can be overwhelmingly tranquil. The back leg of the trail that ascends some 950 ft up to that pass below Knockaffertag can come as a bit of a surprise, but the climb is a gentle one and if taken slowly is one where you can quickly adjust your stride in order to complete it.

As there's a lot of soft ground on this lovely loop, you'll want to pack a pair of gaiters as well as the usual rainproof gear. And there is no real 'high point' to speak of either, but while there is little real climbing to deal with, what this trail does provide is a splendid introductory walk through the mosses and peats and spiky rush-filled wilderness of West Mayo's Atlantic blanket bog landscape. And that alone makes it a walk worth doing.

46. DINGLE WAY
County Kerry, Ireland

Distance: 162 km
Grade: Easy to Moderate
Time: 9 days

One of Ireland's most popular long distance walking trails, the Dingle Way begins in the town of Tralee on the north side of the 'neck' of the Dingle Peninsula, the northernmost of County Kerry's great finger-like projections into the Atlantic. A well-serviced trail, there's never more than a few hours between towns, and there are some positively lonesome stretches of gorgeous, and surprisingly unpopulated, white sand beaches along the way.

Following the N86 out of Tralee the trail passes through Blennerville and crosses the Tralee Ship Canal before a series of backroads take you along the flanks below Slieve Mish, a lovely though compact and quite narrow mountain range full of U-shaped glacial valleys. A marshy section with red sandstone stepping stones leads you past the heads of several glacial valleys and an old reservoir that once provided Tralee with its drinking water. Look out for the Killelton Oratory, a relic of Irish monasticism, before crossing the Finglas River takes you on a descent into Camp village, and the beginning of your 'loop'.

After leaving Camp the trail climbs to a saddle and parallels an impressive ridge between Moanlaur and Knockmore, before descending past the trail's only real forest. After crossing the Emlagh River you will be rewarded with a wonderful view over Inch Beach where scenes from the 1960s film *Ryan's Daughter* were filmed. A cafe here helps make for a welcome rest before a series of small roads past more glacial valleys takes you into the town of Annascaul, the birthplace of Antarctic explorer Tom Crean, whose home – from his retirement until his passing in 1938 – is now the South Pole Inn, a combination of museum and pub.

The trail then descends to sea level along a windswept hillside before passing by a roughly dressed sandstone three-storied tower house – all that remains of the mid-16th-century Minard Castle, made uninhabitable by the severe damage inflicted on it by Cromwellian forces in 1650. Narrow, unpaved and rural roads and secondary roads snake their way through farmlands to the west (don't accidentally wander on to the Tom Crean Trail, a common error) and continue to Lispole with its breathtaking views of Croaghskearda (1,995 ft) and An Cnapan Mor (2,129 ft) before some often marshy farmland trails could see you slipping on your gaiters as you approach Dingle.

Leaving Dingle the trail runs along a beach for the first time at Ventry Harbour, and then the views really open up as you head off on a green road known as Bothar Dorcha (the Dark Road) around Mount Eagle, past Iron Age promontory forts and a multitude of beehive huts, and then get your first glimpses of the lovely Blasket Islands, inhabited until 1953 by an Irish-speaking population who lived in primitive cottages and whose language was the focus of several linguistic studies. Their descendants now live on the Dingle Peninsula, and it is possible to visit Great Blasket Island, the largest in the group, by ferry out of Dunquin Harbour which lies ahead of you – a fascinating side-trip worth factoring in to your itinerary. Out of Dunquin, grassy fields lead to picturesque Clogher Beach and then, after leaving Smerwick Harbour, you'll follow a very impressive 6-km stretch of shore that doesn't end until you reach Ballydavid. This is the centre of an area of uncommercialised local culture that remains uncrowded even during peak summer months when impromptu music sessions by local musicians can occur at any time. There is also a network of excellent local walks here including a section of the Saint's Road and other trails to various archaeological sites.

Brandon Mountain is now looming as the Ballydavid cliffs obscure the ocean to your left, a fact that only serves to increase your focus on the challenge to come. The mountain, at 3,123 ft, is Ireland's second highest and scaling it provides wonderful views back to the Three Sisters, a line of peaks that were the first landfall sighted by Charles Lindbergh at 10.52am on 21 May 1927 on his history-making transatlantic flight. Hiking Brandon Mountain, however, can be a real slog on the way up – a 2,000-ft ascent – particularly if the weather turns nasty, and can be downright dangerous on the way down, making

Photo: Jon Wright

the village of Brandon at the foot of the mountain on the shoreline of Brandon Bay seem a veritable oasis. Brandon is also a *Gaeltacht* village, meaning a place where the Irish language is the dominant vernacular.

From Brandon the trail leads to the village of Clogham on an undulating road inland before returning to the sea at Fermoyle, where it joins with the 14 km of Fermoyle Strand, Ireland's longest beach, before following Scraggane Bay and on into the town of Castlegregory at the end of a small peninsula separating Brandon and Tralee Bays. From Castlegregory you negotiate a flat expanse of bogland before joining the main road into Camp, thus completing the Dingle 'loop', and from there you can follow the Tralee Ship Canal back to Tralee.

The Dingle Way is a coastal walk between sea and mountains. Farms are no-go areas, and where they occur walking is reduced to roads, beaches, or around the margins of heathlands. Mostly there is no right of way. But everywhere you go there is the backdrop of its gloriously glaciated interior mountains, and wherever you look there is colour: fuchsias, honeysuckle, bramble blossoms, emerald-green hills and deep-blue water. There are 4,000- year-old standing stones, ogham stones and beehive huts – more than 2,000 monuments at last count – set amidst an ever-changing light that illuminates this mountainous finger of land that has been home to human beings for more than 6,000 years.

45. FORMARTINE AND BUCHAN WAY

Aberdeenshire, Scotland

Distance: 64 km Dyce to Fraserburgh; 21 km spur Maud to
  Peterhead
Grade: Easy
Time: 4 days

The first stretches of the Formartine and Buchan rail line
were laid through the farmlands north of Aberdeen in 1861,
when a 29-mile section was built linking Dyce with the town
of Mintlaw so that local farmers could more efficiently get
their produce and livestock to market. The line proved so
popular that the following year a 13-mile extension was
opened to Peterhead – a port town since the 16th century and
the easternmost point of mainland Scotland – and in 1865 a
further section was laid to Fraserburgh on the Buchan Coast.
The lines would continue to serve the farming communities
and fishing ports north of Aberdeen until the 1960s, when
Richard Beeching, the chairman of British Railways, in an
age of increasing competition from road transport, wrote
two landmark reports targeting over 2,300 stations and 5,000
miles of rail lines for closure. Not all of his suggestions were
implemented, but most were, including the Peterhead and
Fraserburgh lines, although both continued to carry freight
into the 1970s. Beeching always insisted it was 'surgery, not
mad chopping', but the fact is that the Scottish rail network
was cut asunder by what came to be known as the 'Beeching
Axe'. And it would never be the same again.

What was bad news for rail transport, however, proved
to be, in time, very good news for walkers, especially those
who prefer a flat, easy ramble to energy-sapping ascents.

Photo: Deacon of Pndapetzim

Photo: Anne Burgess

And that is why rail line conversions hold such enormous appeal. There were limits to the climbing capacity of steam locomotives. When gradients are too steep, wheels 'spin' on the track due to insufficient adhesion. So you know that an old railway line isn't going to harbour any real ups or downs. The walking is easy on the Formartine and Buchan Way, but not just on the feet. It's easy on the eye, too.

This lovely rails-to-trails conversion, now an official long distance footpath also open to cyclists and even horse riders providing they have a permit, opened in the early 1990s and extends from Dyce on the outskirts of Aberdeen north to Peterhead and Fraserburgh. It is, not surprisingly perhaps, a straightforward route passing through the towns of Newmachar, Udny, Ellon, Auchnagatt, and Maud – where the route branches off to the north through Strichen and Lonmay to Fraserburgh, and to Peterhead in the east via Old Deer and Mintlaw.

Leaving Dyce you pass over the River Don through farmlands and an old rail cutting at Newmachar then on to a landscape of rolling hills, pastures, and fields of gorse that are ablaze with yellow, and pink rosebay willowherb in summer. Once through Udny the way opens up to cyclists and horse riders as it passes through fields of grazing sheep and past a wind farm before joining a lovely riverside path along the River Ythan taking us into Ellon in the heart of the ancient region of Formartine. Passing under a bridge at Ward Head and through another cutting the views now extend over broad, rich farmlands and on to the lovely old Mill of Elrick which, though now minus its water wheel, still presents a lovely picture with its original stone buildings. A couple of muddy farm tracks are crossed and there's a patch of woodland plantation called – somewhat optimistically – the Grampian Forest, but otherwise you continue into

Maud, and then there's a choice you need to make: either go via Strichen north to Fraserburgh, or to Longside and east to Peterhead.

If Fraserburgh is your goal you can get there in a day, but stock up supplies in Strichen first as there's nothing ahead of you in the way of shops. Before you leave Strichen, allow time to visit the Strichen Stone Circle, a megalithic stone circle destroyed in 1830 and reconstructed in 1960. The trail north of Strichen doubles these days as a farm track used by local farmers. A loch near Newton Wood makes a good rest stop, and overlooking Strichen is the Mormond Hill White Horse, thought to have been cut in the late 1790s by a local officer whose horse was shot out from under him in a battle with the Dutch in 1794. A series of platforms, bridges and linesman's huts are passed and then Fraserburgh Bay and its bustling working harbour – Europe's largest shellfish port – finally comes into view.

Should Peterhead be your destination, you will head out to Bridgend, then past the crumbling walls that are all that remain of the Cistercian monastery of Deer Abbey, founded in 1219. If so inclined and not pressed for time you can take a detour into the charming town of Old Deer, with its main street – Abbey Street – a lovely blend of 18th- and 19th-century buildings. Back on the Way you go through woodlands and down the centre of Mintlaw before an expanse of wide, flat farmland – with the old rail line, your unmistakable guide, all but disappearing in a straight line ahead of you – takes you into Peterhead.

The Formartine and Buchan Way not only provides a rural retreat for walkers – as well as containing many sections that are wheelchair accessible – it has also become an important corridor for wildlife including foxes, deer, badgers, weasels, partridges and pheasant. It links secluded forests and

THE 50 GREATEST WALKS OF THE WORLD

marshlands, and continues to breathe new life into a tiny and easily overlooked corner of rural Scotland.

44. COTSWOLD WAY
Gloucestershire, Somerset, England

Distance: 164 km
Grade: Moderate
Time: 8–10 days

The Cotswolds, as those who are aware will be only too happy to tell you, are not, in fact, hills. They are an escarpment – the Cotswold Edge – a line of high country almost 160 km in length that runs from England's southwest up to its midlands. Like escarpments everywhere it is a region of tilted rock – on one side a gentle slope eastwards towards the Oxfordshire Plain and the Thames Valley, while on the other side a far more pronounced and abrupt westward slope down to the plain of the Severn Valley. Composed of oolitic limestone laid down 150 million years ago this rock, composed of small, round grains, is not white like limestone tends to be but is instead a lovely ethereal pale gold; easily split and delightfully weather-resistant, it hardens over time. So why does this matter? Because you see it everywhere here, not just in the ground but in many of the buildings you pass on the Cotswold Way in villages that are the equal in beauty of any in England – places like Chipping Campden, Stanton, Broadway and Stanway – villages capable of ruining itineraries because you can't drag yourself away from them. Golden coloured vignettes that flicker in a golden-hued landscape. 'As if they know the trick', wrote J. B. Priestley, 'of keeping the lost sunlight of centuries glimmering about them'.

Inaugurated as a national trail in April 2007 after first being mooted by the Rambler's Association in the 1950s, the Cotswold Way runs northeast out of Bath and is a trail of ups and downs as it meanders along the western rim of the scarp, providing glimpses of market towns far below and then heading down to them on switchbacks through a world of wild roses, drystone walls and fields of bluebells, with kestrels above and cropped turf below. You can walk it north-south or south-north – both are equally well signed – though the going is a tad more 'inclined' for the northbound walker. Walking north, however, means the very best of the Cotswolds will be waiting for you as a sort of 'grand finale'.

Leaving Bath, the first segment of the Cotswold Way is a long day's walk to Old Sodbury, just below and to the west of the escarpment, and already you're being seduced by the scent of wild garlic and the playful shadows cast by beech woodlands. At Penn Hill just beyond Weston (once a separate village to Bath, now swallowed up by it) and Kelston Round Hill (714 ft) the views really begin to open up and hint at the broad panoramas to come: the Severn Estuary and the Severn Bridges, the Black Mountains of southeast Wales, May Hill on the Gloucestershire/Herefordshire border, the jagged Malvern Hills, the Vale of Evesham, and Cleeve Hill.

But it's the villages and towns along the way – and some off the way you really need to see, like Cheltenham – that make this walk what it is, a concentration of natural and built history few English trails can match. There is Wotton-under-Edge, tucked beneath the edge of the escarpment with Nibley Hill over it; the old textile mills of Stroud; gorgeous Snowshill with its ancient cottages, 19th-century church and village

Photo: Rwendland

green set in the hills above Broadway; and there is Broadway itself, with its chestnut trees and wisteria-draped cottages built of limestone that is positively yellow. While in Broadway you also need to make the ascent to Broadway Tower, a folly completed in 1798, a place of inspiration for William Morris, the founder of the Arts and Crafts architectural style, and a high point from which the views – some say into sixteen counties - would be difficult to exaggerate. Finally the trail comes to an end in Chipping Campden, a wool trading centre in the Middle Ages now with a gorgeous High Street of terraced 14th- to 17th-century buildings and without doubt the Cotswold's most elegant town.

You can bring a tent here if you want, but camping facilities are somewhat scarce though some B&Bs do allow it with prior permission. Much better, though, to rest in comfort so as not to allow aching limbs to distract you from the beauty around you as you walk this idyllic plateau that is a part of one enormous slab of limestone that stretches all the way from Dorset to Yorkshire – England's largest continuous geological feature, sprinkled with villages clad in the very rock that made it all possible.

43. HERRIOT WAY
North Yorkshire, England

Distance: 88 km
Grade: Easy
Time: 4–5 days

James Alfred 'Alf' Wight (Herriot was a pen name) was born

in Sunderland in County Durham in 1916 and grew up in Glasgow where he attended Glasgow Veterinary College, graduating as a veterinary surgeon in 1939 at the age of 23. The following year he took a veterinary position in the Yorkshire town of Thirsk, a traditional market town and now gateway to the Yorkshire Dales National Park. Alf Wight would remain in the Yorkshire Dales and the heather-clad moorlands of the North York Moors for the rest of his life. He achieved world-wide fame as an author in 1972 with the publication of his best-selling book *All Creatures Great and Small* which, along with his numerous other titles, tapped into the public's seemingly insatiable desire to read about his lifetime of animal-related incidents and anecdotes.

The Herriot Way passes through Wensleydale on the east side of the Pennines, famous for its cheese and – for fans of Richard III – Middleham Castle, the childhood home of the hunchback king; and through the green meadows, drystone walls and glacier-cut slopes of Swaledale – a land of wild flowers, waterfalls, and the dark brooding moors of fiction. These are the dales that form the backdrop to Herriot's simple tales, what he called 'my little cat-and-dog stories', through which you pass on a walk that is itself something of a rarity – a multi-day hike that is also circular. Beginning at its considered starting point in Aysgarth (although Grinton or Hawes also make acceptable starting points) it can be walked anti-clockwise, which will take you out across open moorlands towards Apedale, or clockwise, following the River Ure past rolling meadows, paralleling an old rail line and arriving in Askrigg.

Presuming you choose the anti-clockwise option there are four stages to your journey: Aysgarth to Hawes (21 km), Hawes to Keld (21 km), Keld to Grinton (23 km), and Grinton to Aysgarth Falls (20 km). From Aysgarth you follow

Photo: Kreuzschnabel

the River Ure past the Aysgarth Falls and through farmland to the 14th-century Bolton Castle, a wonderful example of a quadrangular castle which was a temporary home/refuge to Mary, Queen of Scots after she fled Scotland in the aftermath of the Battle of Langside. A steep climb over open moorland then takes you to Apedale and Apedale Head, a rather desolate former mining area. A track over expanses of heather skirts Grinton Hill before descending into the town of Grinton, known locally as the 'Cathedral of the Dales' because its St Andrew's Church, largely a 15th-century rebuild over earlier 12th- and 14th-century remains, was the only church serving all of upper Swaledale for hundreds of years. (Note for Herriot fans: this is the church that was featured in the *All Creatures Great and Small* episode 'Brotherly Love').

Leaving Grinton you pass through the pastures of the Swale to the market town of Reeth, home to another well-known author: Ruby Ferguson, whose romantic writings were so beloved by the Queen Mother that she was invited to dinner at Buckingham Palace. Once through Heelaugh you're into some of the finest heather moorlands in England before dropping down into the town of Keld, at the crossroads of two of England's most-travelled long distance trails – the Coast to Coast, and the Pennine Way. Here you follow the Pennine Way to the picturesque and unspoilt village of Thwaite, before girding yourself for the climb up Great Shunner Fell, the Yorkshire Dales' third-highest mountain (716 m) with the Pennine Way passing right over its summit on a flagstone path.

From here it's a straightforward descent into Hawes, Yorkshire's highest trading town, first recorded as a marketplace in 1307 and home to the Wensleydale Creamery of Wensleydale cheese fame; the method for making this was first brought here by French Cistercian monks in 1150 and was continued by local farmers after the Dissolution of the Monasteries in 1540. While in Hawes also be sure not to miss Gayle Mill, a restored 19th-century sawmill with Victorian machinery still driven by water-powered turbines. Back on the Pennine Way you make your way to Hardraw (old English for 'Shepherd's dwelling') and the Hardraw Force waterfall, at 33 m England's largest single-drop waterfall, within the grounds of the 13th-century Green Dragon Inn and its public bar that, it is claimed, dates to the 14th century.

Hay meadows, farmland, and quiet laneways then lead you into Askrigg, the 'Darrowby' of the television series, before following the banks of the River Ure through the Wensleydale Valley and to a final, short ascent back to Aysgarth. And the circle is complete.

For lovers of the *All Creatures Great and Small* television series there are of course the countless urban sites that, despite being otherwise a tad nondescript, will leave you suitably breathless and likely add hours to any Herriot Way circumnavigation: places like Finghall Railway Station (aka Darrowby Station), the Church of St Mary and St John in Hardraw (the Darrowby church), the Kings Arms Hotel in Askrigg (The Drovers' Arms), Cringley House, now renamed Skeldale House B&B, also in Askrigg (the building was used as the exterior for the veterinary practice), the village green in Redmire (the Darrowby bus stop), and the road between Feetham and Langthwaite Bridge, seen in the series' opening title sequence. And of course you'll want to visit the marvellous World of James Herriot Museum located in his former surgery at 23 Kirkgate in Thirsk, the real Skeldale House.

The Herriot Way can be walked in winter, too, depending upon how much snow falls on its higher elevations. The route between Aysgarth and Hawes is low enough and rarely is snow an impediment there, but the trail over the gently sloping Great Shunner Fell could slow one's progress. Most winters, however, all you're likely to get is just wet.

As a memoir of these four lovely days you might consider purchasing a copy of his book *James Herriot's Yorkshire* (1979), a sumptuous and very personal pictorial tour through the dales so beloved of the author that is beautifully photographed by Derry Brabbs, one of England's finest photographers.

42. BURREN WAY
County Clare, Ireland

Distance: 114 km
Grade: Moderate
Time: 7 days

'Burren' comes from the Gaelic word *Boireann* which means a rocky place. And so it is. The Burren in Ireland's northern County Clare is a vast area of exposed carboniferous limestone pavements cut by thousands of parallel 'grikes' – vertical fissures up to 0.5 m wide. Ancient travellers used to call them 'fertile rocks' – channels cut by acidic waters that went to work along the lines of greatest weakness and which now grow limestone-loving plants such as foxgloves and rock roses and lichens such as lugwort and Parmeliella, all in a region formed from the sediments of an ancient inland sea. One of the largest karst systems – dissolved limestone – in Europe, the Burren pavement covers a 130-square-km region near the famous Cliffs of Moher with views out to the

Aran Islands and over Galway Bay. It is also home to a unique concentration of Neolithic and early Christian ruins and monuments including more than 400 ring forts, 60 Stone Age wedge tombs and dolmens, and a variety of churches and monasteries. It is an ancient landscape, chiselled out by the retreating glaciers of the Ice Age, added to by man and not left alone by nature which has clung on here to produce a varied and hardy landscape through which passes one of Ireland's most fascinating trails – the Burren Way.

The Burren Way is a National Waymarked Trail in County Clare that begins in the town of Lahinch on Liscannor Bay and ends in Corofin, a small village on the River Fergus. The trail takes in the best of what this surreal landscape has to offer and is best done over seven days – days that will be spent on a variety of near-empty tarmac roads, old cattle trails, forestry roads and green trails that will take you through a unique habitat. A designated Special Area of Conservation, the limestone plateau of the Burren is, indeed, surprisingly fertile, helped along by a temperate climate, and is a meeting place for Arctic and alpine plants that thrive side by side with Mediterranean woodland plants that grow here despite the absence of large trees to provide them with shade.

There are several trail options you can take when you come here but the most popular route that will take you through the Burren's limestone heart is a seven-day hike that departs from Liscannor and follows coastal tracks around Liscannor Bay to the southernmost point of the famous Cliffs of Moher at the start of the 13-km-long Cliffs of Moher Coastal Walk. This is one of the most majestic coastal paths in Europe and will take you into the town of Doolin where you can have a look inside Doolin Cave at one of Ireland's most unique natural attractions – the 'Great Stalactite' – at 23 ft long, the Northern Hemisphere's longest free-standing stalactite.

Photo: psyberartist

From Doolin you head off on a gentle climb along the flank of 344-m, shale-capped Slieve Elva past Ballynalacken Castle, which provides lovely views over the Burren and the mountains of Connemara, before ending the day on the wonderfully wide sandy beach at Fanore on the Ballyvaughan–Doolin road. For a nice half-day's diversion you can do an 18-km loop walk out of Fanore up to lonely Black Head with its lighthouse and more views, this time over Galway Bay, and then on down an ancient path into the Gleninagh Valley past a Celtic stone fort near the Caher River before returning to Fanore.

Then it's along more clifftops to Ballyvaughan via the 16th-century Newtown Castle, and from Ballyvaughan you enter the Burren's limestone landscape, following dry-stone walls past time-worn Celtic ruins. On the last day, the most secluded, you'll walk a trail above Castletown River past ancient tombs and ringforts skirting the boundary of Inchiquin Lough, a limestone lake famous for its resident brown trout, pike and perch, before ending your walk in Corofin, situated on the very edge of the expanse of limestone pavements, the so-called 'Gateway to the Burren'.

Spring is the preferred season to walk the trail thanks to a profusion of wildflowers and orchids, but you'll need an eye for detail here if you're to get the most out of this outwardly lunar-like landscape. If you put in the research, however, you'll discover the Burren is a wonderland of underground drainage caves such as Aillwee Cave near Ballyvaughan, with its kilometre of passageways, underground river and waterfall and the remains of bears which have led some to guess it may have been the last bear den in Ireland. It may also be Ireland's oldest cave, with calcite samples dating back more than 350,000 years.

To come to the Burren in County Clare is to walk through

a region that was once a forest and is now a fissured world of limestone, lakes that long ago ceased to be, underground caves and rivers, wild orchids, terraced hillsides, springs, hidden wells – and a trail that helps bring it all to life.

41. DUBLIN MOUNTAINS WAY
Dublin Mountains, Ireland

Distance: 43 km
Grade: Moderate
Time: 2 days

It began in the 1980s – a slow but steadily building chorus of Dubliners calling for the establishment of a proper network of walking trails through the Wicklow Mountains through County Dublin. In (eventual) response to this, the Dublin Mountains Partnership was formed in 2008, and once established lost no time in gathering the support of various local councils, as well as a small number of private landowners, to bring the dream of a 'Dublin Mountains Way' to fruition. Existing trails soon began to be upgraded, a sleepered bridge was added at the summit of Tibradden Mountain to protect existing heathland, and more than 300 people from volunteer groups spread out through the Wicklow Mountains like ants, building stone stairways, clearing trails, building bog bridges, and adding water management features to prevent trail erosion. The first section was opened in June 2009, and within two years of the first sods being turned, the Dublin Mountains Way officially opened on 31 October 2010.

Photo: Joe King

A long distance, fully waymarked trail that takes you through the mountains from Shankill west to Tallaght and with a total ascent of around 1,100 m, the trail begins in Brady's Pub in the heart of Shankill village (well ok, the trail actually begins on the main street beside Brady's Pub, but why split hairs?) and continues through the suburbs (don't worry, the views are coming) to Rathmichael and the Rathmichael Cross, once a marker between two 12th-century churches and one of many so-called Fassaroe Crosses, unusual in that it depicts a crucifixion scene on both its faces. From there you enter Rathmichael Wood, a mixed coniferous and broadleaf woodland which opens up to lovely views across to Bray Head. The trail then skirts Carrickgollogan Wood, and it's well worth the climb to its 276-m summit, from where you'll be able to see the Lead Mine Chimney Flue, once a part of the Ballycorus Lead Mine which operated from 1807 to 1913, with its distinctive external stone spiral staircase, the only one of its kind in Ireland. For a close-up view of the tower you can take the 2-km detour on the Lead Mines Way.

Now you make your way via Barnaslingan Wood to Barnaslingan Hill (781 ft) and its view over The Scalp, a narrow glacial valley formed during the last Ice Age and a designated Area of Special Scientific Interest. Emerging on to Enniskerry Road the trail parallels the R117 into the small village of Kilternan, after which you take the R116 and begin the climb up to Glencullen, one of Ireland's highest-altitude villages, where you'll find Johnnie Fox's Pub, which also claims to be the country's highest pub – though this is disputed by various other high-altitude establishments. The pub has an interesting history though, and was used as a meeting place by members of the 1916 Rebellion. Outside of town on the slope of Three Rock Mountain the trail passes by a Bronze Age (c. 1,700 BCE) wedge tomb excavated in the 1940s and known locally as the 'giant's grave'.

More road walking, this time along Ballyedmonduff Road up to Ticknock Forest and the summit of Three Rock Mountain and on to Two Rock Mountain, the trail's high point at 1,759 ft where you'll find the remains of a Neolithic passage grave. A ridge walk to Tibradden Mountain (1,532 ft) then descends through a forest of oak, beech, Scots pine and Sitka spruce before passing along the north slope of Cruagh Mountain and down a series of minor roads into the Glenasmole Valley, a lovely slender gorge, home to green-winged and small-white orchids and a declared Special Area of Conservation. Following the Upper Reservoir of the Bohernabreena Waterworks and the River Dodder (dammed in the 1880s) down to the Lower Reservoir, the trail continues along the Dodder through housing estates and into Tallaght's Sean Walsh Memorial Park, an oasis of landscaped parklands, where the trail ends.

40. ROB ROY WAY
Stirlingshire and Perthshire, Scotland

Distance: 127 km
Grade: Moderate
Time: 6–7 days

The third son of Donald Glas MacGregor of Glengyle, Robert 'Rob' Roy MacGregor was born in 1671 into one of Scotland's most ancient families, a family that in 1589 killed a royal forester (a man who had hanged a few MacGregors for poaching) and a family that had by the early 1600s been reduced to the status of 'outlaws', a status that was reinforced by William of Orange decades later. Long before Rob Roy was born, then, he was predestined to be an outlaw despite for a time making a decent living in the 'honourable' highlands pursuit of cattle rustling. In 1711 he was branded an outlaw by the 1st Duke of Montrose, to whom he was unable to repay a large debt. In the Jacobite rebellion of 1715, his land and cattle confiscated and name blackened, he led the MacGregor clan in a war against the hated English, was captured twice, and each time made a dramatic escape. In 1725 he turned himself in and was pardoned in 1727, within days of being sent away on a transport ship to Barbados. But his fight was done. Rob Roy returned home, converted to Catholicism, and lived out his days in relative anonymity, passing away in Inverlochie on 28 December 1734.

If you intend walking the Rob Roy Way you should come knowing something of the man whose posthumous mix of myth and legend led to the trail's creation in 2002. It begins in the market town of Drymen in Loch Lomond and Trossachs National Park from where it enters Loch Ard Forest by Loch Ard, considered one of Scotland's prettiest lochs, and on to the village of Aberfoyle. The next stop is Callander, the 'Gateway to the Highlands' with the backdrop of Callander Crags rising to 1,000 ft and offering a beautiful diversion into its elevated trail-filled woodlands and views over the Forth Valley. Descending to Loch Venachar and into the very heart of the land Rob Roy so loved, follow National Cycle Route 7 on a shortish day's walk to Strathyre along a disused rail line and past the dramatic Falls of Leny, close to the village of Kilmahog.

It's highland walking in full swing now as you pass the Falls of Dochart at the end of Loch Tay and into the town of Killin and the must-visit ruins of the L-shaped Finlarig Castle, a tower house built by the Campbells of Breadalbane and visited by Rob Roy in 1713, but which is now in a perilous state of repair. You should also allow time to visit Rob Roy's grave at Balquhidder, although this will add around 6 km to your day's walk. Leaving Killin you'll skirt beautiful Loch Breaclaich and find yourself immersed in the wooded hills above Loch Tay and the Tay River Valley before descending to Ardtalnaig. Some rough paths and gorge walking follow as you make your way to Aberfeldy, where a visit to Dewar's World of Whisky is recommended, and lastly you'll pass through open moorlands on the approach to Pitlochry, which has been 'on the map' ever since Queen Victoria visited it in 1842 and which became an 'official' tourist town with the arrival of the railway in 1863. A town rich in stone-built Victorian buildings, the trail takes you on a dramatic crossing of the suspension bridge over the River Tummel before reaching the end of the Rob Roy Way at the northwest corner of Pitlochry's Memorial Park.

Walking the Rob Roy Way not only gets you deep into the heart of the highlands, it provides an opportunity to separate the man from the substantial myths that surround him. In 1723 an account of the still living Robert MacGregor's life, titled *Highland Rogue*, overlaid with half-truths and a lot of bogus history, has been attributed to Daniel Defoe, the author of *Robinson Crusoe*. Much later, in 1817, Sir Walter Scott wrote *Rob Roy*, published anonymously and in three volumes describing a glamorised 'Scottish Robin Hood'. These accounts, both eloquently written, only served to muddy the historical waters surrounding Rob Roy, waters which you, as a journeyman on the Rob Roy Way, now have a chance to navigate for yourself.

Photo: Phillip Capper

39. THAMES PATH
Cotswolds to Thames Barrier, England

Distance: 296 km
Grade: Easy
Time: 12–14 days

It began as little more than a drainage line in the Palaeocene epoch 58 million years ago. Some 500,000 years ago, long before there ever was a North Sea, it was a tributary of the Rhine when its course began to be altered and turned southwards by the Anglian Ice Sheet, helped along by overspill from ice-dammed lakes. Its signature stacked-terrace sediments – remnants of former flood plains – began to be laid down, providing our modern world with perhaps its finest window into the environment of the later Pleistocene era. Hippos, elephants and rhinoceros roamed its banks 125,000 years ago, when it flowed through what is now Trafalgar Square, and Ice Age fossils of mammals and plants have been found throughout this valley that has been a route for human movement for tens of thousands of years. When you walk alongside the River Thames on the Thames Path between its source in the Cotswolds and the magnificent Thames Barrier in east London, as you pass by its 45 locks, 58 islands, 134 bridges and 20 major tributaries, you are not just tracing a line along a riverbank. You are walking through a geological time tunnel that echoes the formation of England itself.

The 296-km (184-mile)-long Thames Path was first suggested in 1948, and was opened in 1996, and though it can be walked in either direction most prefer to begin at its source in the Cotswolds. It begins as a trickle in a field 107 m (356 ft) above sea level at a spring beneath an ageing ash tree, known as Thames Head, near the town of Kemble, where you will find an official marker. This site, however, is disputed, with the Ordnance Survey placing its true source at nearby Trewsbury Mead while others insist it begins at Seven Springs, a tiny hamlet south of Cheltenham. The marker, however, represents a logical enough starting point and as you proceed south you can clearly see the infant river's footprint – a V-shaped dry, grassy gully that continues on till you reach Lyd Well, a Roman well and active spring that gushes water from its subterranean source and provides the river's first noticeable body of surface water.

The first of an endless array of hamlets and villages you'll encounter is Ewen, an old Saxon word meaning 'source of a river', where the Thames broadens to a couple of metres in width – though still shallow enough to cross on foot. When the river reaches Ashton Keynes, 11 km from the source, it divides into several streams with the main flow paralleling the High Road and strengthened thanks to the intervention of the Swill Brook tributary. In truth the Thames here is really a tributary of Swill Brook, which is much larger at this junction. But Swill Brook's identity is swallowed up as its waters merge with its famous cousin.

The river continues through the myriad lakes of the Cotswold Water Park (man-made lakes mostly, thanks to the area's history of gravel extraction) and skirts the National Nature Reserve of North Meadow before entering Cricklade, which was fortified by King Alfred to protect it against Viking incursions and is the only Wiltshire town on the river. It is here that the River Churn, yet another claimant to being the Thames's source, joins the river. From Cricklade it is on to the town of Castle Eaton with its lovely ancient thoroughfare,

Photo: Buca

The Street, and its 17th- to 19th-century buildings that you are encouraged to walk down as the Thames Path diverts at this point away from the river, through town, and on to the farmlands to the east before rejoining the river near the town of Kempsford. A bridleway takes you into Upper Inglesham, where you might want to take a taxi or bus to Inglesham rather than walk along a busy A361. Just be sure not to leave Inglesham without seeing the delightfully unaltered 11th-century Church of St John the Baptist with its atmospheric Jacobean boxed pews.

The Round House between Inglesham and Lechlade, originally built as accommodation for canal lock-keepers with their horses on the ground floor and the keepers above, is where the Thames and Severn Canal joins the river, and it is from here that the river becomes navigable. Lechlade was a bustling port in the early 1800s when in excess of a dozen 65-ton barges at a time carried salt (and cheese, bricks, meat, lead, animal skins, timber and flour) along what was known as the 'Old Salt Way' to the markets in Oxford and London. Walking into Lechlade you leave the river again after crossing the Ha'penny Bridge, a lovely old stone bridge. It is here where the rivers Leach and Coln enter the Thames, adding considerably to its depth, and widening it to over 16 m.

The next section from Lechlade to Newbridge, at just over 26 km, is the Thames Path's longest slog. Here you'll find 6 of the river's 45 non-tidal locks including St John's Lock – at 71.5 m (234 ft) above sea level, the river's highest – and a succession of concrete pill boxes built as a line of defence against a German invasion that never came. This section is a lovely ramble through the open country that is the river's flat flood plain. The horizons are wide here, with hedges and meadows grazed by sheep and cattle and Chimney Meadows Nature Reserve, an important habitat for ground-nesting birds, covering 250 hectares of wetland meadows in the Upper Thames Floodplain. On your way to Newbridge you'll pass over the oldest bridge on the Thames – the Radcot Bridge built around the year 1200 and reconstructed after the Wars of the Roses – with its lovely pointed arches of Taynton stone.

The river broadens still further at Newbridge, yet despite the resultant increase in river traffic the path to Oxford remains pleasantly rural. Just make sure you take a diversion to the village of Kelmscott to see Kelmscott Manor, the summer home of William Morris, and his grave at Kelmscott Church. Soon the path again leaves the river, this time at the tiny hamlet of Bablock Hythe only 8 km west of Oxford. Skirting Wytham Woods to the city's north the path goes under the city's ring road, past the remains of Godstow Abbey (circa 1133) and through Port Meadow, that wonderful expanse of common land grazing pastures still populated largely by horses and cattle that hasn't been ploughed in thousands of years.

The path to Abingdon, an attractive market town with the remains of its wonderful 7th-century Benedictine abbey, is where the River Ock enters the Thames. Crossing to the river's southern bank on the Abingdon Bridge you then make a series of twists and turns alongside an increasingly meandering river and arrive in Clifton Hampton with its wealth of thatched Elizabethan cottages, and Wallingford, which in the days prior to bridges offered the most convenient fording point on the river north of London. Then it's on to the Goring Gap, a narrow route through the chalk of the Chiltern Hills cut by the river during the last Ice Age which constricts the otherwise broad valley and its river and draws them in like the eye of a needle. The tranquillity of the Goring Gap soon gives way to the city of Reading (although the path keeps to the less urbanised north of the city), and from there it's on to Sonning with its lovely hump-backed bridge, and Henley-on-Thames, site of the Royal Regatta.

Numerous villages and points of interest here include Bisham, recorded in Domesday Book with its All Saints Parish Church and altar that is so close to the river that floodwaters have been known to lap at its base; Marlow, a Georgian town with its graceful 19th-century suspension bridge and the wooded slopes of Winter Hill on the opposite bank providing one of the path's most picturesque backdrops; and the watery expanse of Cock Marsh, 46 acres of water meadows near Cookham that has been common land since 1272. Between Cookham and Boulter's Lock, just out of sight behind a rising hillside of beech, lies the grandeur of Cliveden House, which has played host to almost every British monarch since George I. Now one of the world's finest hotels it costs nothing to leave the path and take a leisurely stroll through its immaculate gardens.

Windsor is next, which means not only a stop at Windsor Castle but a lovely walk through the castle's Home Park, the beginnings of which date to the 1600s. By now green space is becoming harder to find on the Thames Path, although the grasslands and meadows of Runnymede and the Home Park of Hampton Court Palace will make one want to linger. At Teddington the river becomes tidal and it is here, the site of the river's longest lock, where you've a choice of which riverbank to follow; or you can even criss-cross it using one of the increasingly frequent bridges as you make your way to Putney. The south bank will take you through Petersham Meadows, the Old Deer Park in Richmond and the Royal Botanic Gardens at Kew; the north bank offers Marble Hill Park and Dukes Meadows.

The heart of London is now before you, and the choices

continue: the promenades at Wandsworth and Battersea Park on the south bank; or Hurlingham Park, Westminster and the Houses of Parliament on the north bank. Greenwich soon beckons, and from there to the O2 Centre – past working wharves, dilapidated piers and the Millennium Dome – where the iconic gleaming hoods of the Thames Barrier, the finish line, appear.

To walk the Thames Path is to come to an understanding of what it means to be English. Its waters gave birth to London, and to the rural landscapes of thatched cottages, hedges and village greens that stretch from the Cotswolds to the city. Runnymede, Greenwich, Hampton Court, Windsor, Oxford, Eton, the Tower, Westminster Abbey. Is it any wonder it has been labelled a 'museum of Englishness'?

38. ANGLESEY COASTAL PATH
Anglesey Island, Wales

Distance: 212 km
Grade: Moderate
Time: 10–12 days

Don't think that walking this trail, almost all of which is set within the boundaries of a designated Area of Outstanding Natural Beauty, is going to be a doddle just because it is classified 'coastal'. Setting out from Holyhead you have an energy-sapping 13,695 ft of accumulated elevation gain in front of you, the product of a geologically complex coastline that has long been the focal point for countless field trips by schools, colleges, and university geology departments; a coastline that in 2009 led to the island being admitted to the European Geoparks Network, and then to the Global Geoparks Network the following year. If you're the sort of person who can't travel without a book tucked under your arm, a copy of Edward Greenly's *The Geology of Anglesey* (1919) wouldn't go amiss. Greenly was the first to coin the phrase Mona Complex, a term he applied to the Precambrian rocks that cover more than half of the island's interior. His field work was so accurate that his two-volume work still remains a standard source of reference.

In fact you might want to build a few extra days into your itinerary just to allow for the geological wonders you'll be passing on the way, and maybe even pick up a laminated 'Geotrails' map from the Geopark Visitor Centre in the Old Watch Tower at Porth Amlwch, so you'll be better able to appreciate the tortured processes that went into creating Wales's largest island.

Anglesey Island, it turns out, has some serious geological bragging rights: more than 100 rock types, four eras and a dozen Geological periods spanned, and more than 1.8 billion years of earth's history on show. As a result there are a variety of 'Geo Trails', any or all of which are worth taking while you are there, trails such as the one on to Llanddwyn Island, a tidal island off Anglesey's west coast connected to the island except at the highest of tides. Llanddwyn contains an entire plate tectonic record, including Precambrian pillow lavas that shine a light on the creation of the ocean floor. There are the spectacular folded schists (layers of crystalline, metamorphic rock) at South Stack lighthouse, the limestone coast around Penmon, a 'thrust fault' at Carmel Head, and the world's premier 'melange' site (rocks jumbled together at the edge of a destructive plate margin) at Cemaes Bay. There are the Red Wharf Bay's brachiopod-rich limestones formed long ago in warm tropical seas, and the rare blue schist at Llanfairpwll, turned blue under enormous pressure deep in the earth's crust. All this and more threatens to significantly extend the journey of the well-informed walker.

The official starting point for the walk is outside the 16th-century St Cybi's church in the centre of Holyhead on Holy Island. Walking a clockwise route you cross a low-lying path around the Alaw Estuary to Church Bay, after which you're immediately immersed in one of the most remote areas on the entire trail, with rock-strewn coves merging with twisted, folded cliffs and the offshore islands at Ynys y Fydlyn. After the pretty village of Cemaes come the dizzying cliffs of Porth Llanlleiana and Porth Cynfor. Then comes quaint Amlwch Port and the sandy expanse of Dulas Estuary. Continuing down the east coast and passing through Moelfre, which didn't receive its first street lights until after the Second World War, a series of dramatic limestone cliffs takes you down to Benllech and on to Red Wharf Bay. A serious stretch of shoreline walking follows before an ascent to the flat-topped limestone hill of Bwrdd Arthur (an old hill fort prior to and during the Roman invasion), then there's more shoreline walking with views to the Cameddau Mountains and the Menai Strait.

The town Beaumaris at the eastern entrance to the Menai Strait, which can trace its origins to its development as a Viking port, is a must-do stopover if only to visit the ruins of magnificent Beaumaris Castle, begun in 1295 when Edward I ordered the construction of a moated castle as part of his campaign to conquer northern Wales. Even though work on the castle was abandoned after 1330 due to a lack of funds, and it was left incomplete with its south gate open to the sea to allow for resupply by ship, it remains

Photo: Ton 1959

one of Britain's finest examples of symmetrical, concentric castle architecture. UNESCO went as far to describe it as an 'artistic achievement', lauding it for its 'walls within walls' design and the beauty of its proportions.

Although the next section of the coastal path involves a lot of road walking, the trail from Beaumaris to Llanfairpwll has nice elevated views over the Menai Strait, plus it dips under the historic Menai Suspension Bridge. Designed by civil engineer Thomas Telford it was the world's biggest suspension bridge when completed in 1826 and slashed travel time to London for farmers who no longer had to negotiate the waters of the Menai Strait. Wooded farmlands parallel the path's flattest section to Moel-y-don to Dwyran, with views south to mainland Snowdonia and Caernarfon Castle. The route's southernmost section passes through a nature reserve with conifers and sand dunes and around the Ffraw Estuary into Aberffraw, the capital of the Kingdom of Gwynedd from 860 to 1170 CE and the political hub of medieval Wales.

The trail is seriously exposed and could benefit from a little more wooded cover, especially in summer. But it is a forlorn hope. Forests here are at a premium. By the 13th century Anglesey Island, with its concept of shared, open-field agriculture, had become 'Mon Mam Cymru' – the 'granary of Wales'. A laudable title, but one that came at a price. Just 4 per cent of its deciduous woodlands now remain.

A series of low, rocky cliffs out of Aberffraw lead to Barclodiad y Gawres, a Neolithic cruciform passage grave excavated in 1952–53. Then a vast expanse of sandy beaches and low-lying farmlands takes you on to Holy Island off Anglesey's west coast, so named because of its large number of standing stones and burial chambers. From Holy Island an interesting coastal landscape of inlets, coves and colourful sea cliffs follows, including Bwa Gwyn (the 'White Arch'), a glorious natural arch of white quartzite criss-crossed by a network of dramatic fractures. Traversing the sandy bay around Trearddur you climb the cliffs on your approach (via a footbridge) to South Stack lighthouse, built in 1809 on tiny South Stack Rock to provide a guiding light to ships plying the treacherous Dublin–Holyhead–Liverpool sea route. You'll want to linger here if you're a birder, too. South Stack is home to thousands of guillemots, razorbills, and even a sprinkling of delightful puffins.

For a fine perspective over Holy Island you can climb to the summit of Holyhead Mountain (220 m), which provides fabulous 360 degree views before descending down into Holyhead, and the end of a journey through space – and time.

37. RIVER AYR WAY
East and South Ayrshire, Scotland

Distance: 66 km
Grade: Easy
Time: 3 days

The River Ayr Way, Scotland's first 'sea to source' trail, was opened in 2006. Within a year, in excess of 10,000 people had come to walk all or part of it. The path begins as an overflow out of Glenbuck Loch, an artificial reservoir on the Lanarkshire/Ayrshire border created in the late 1780s to provide a source of water for a series of cotton mills at nearby Catrine. A popular river for anglers who come here looking for salmon, sea trout, brown trout, grayling and stickleback,

Photo: Chris Wimbush

Photo: Ayrtime

it flows westwards through moorlands and past various relics to the Industrial Age as it steadily grows in strength beside you, picking up the waters of Greenock Water, the Lugar Water, the Water of Fail and the Water of Coyle, until it reaches the coastal town of Ayr, and empties into the Firth of Clyde.

There's a real sense of accomplishment when you trace the entire course of a river, from an often innocuous source and on past its adjoining streams and tributaries, all the way to its inevitable merging with the sea. Walked over two or three stages on an easy waymarked path the River Ayr Way is short enough to complete over a long weekend or even on a two-day weekend if you get early starts.

Leaving Glenbuck Loch the trail leads on to a section of the old Caledonian Railway, past the abandoned Glenbuck Station railway platform and past a still operating open-cut mine into Kames, where a circuit to the summit of Cairn Table (1,945 ft) is an option if you feel like adding a moderate ascent to an otherwise easy, flat ramble.

A highlight on the trail are the woodlands of the Ayr Gorge in the Ayr Gorge Wildlife Refuge, a mix of steep ravines and sandstone cliffs covered in beech, larch and oak and one of Ayrshire's most precious ancient woodland environments. Declared a Site of Special Scientific Interest Ayr Gorge is home to a wealth of invertebrates including spiders and beetles, and five species of bats. Birdlife includes warblers, Spotted Flycatchers and Bullfinches. Replanted birch trees here have done so well they've had to be thinned to provide enough light and space for other species. Airds Moss is another ecological treat, an area of blanket or 'featherbed' bogs, a designated Special Area of Conservation and home to grouse, hen harriers and peregrine falcons. It's also where, in 1680, Richard Cameron, the leader of the militant

Presbyterian group known as the Covenanters opposed to Stuart attempts to control the Church of Scotland, was killed by English dragoons.

The path is never too far away from remnants, ruins, and still intact structures that echo the region's industrial – and inventive – past. Just outside Kames the path runs right over an early 18th-century attempt at road surfacing by a local man, John MacAdam. After leaving Catrine on the way to Mauchline the path rises above the river and passes through a lovely wooded valley before passing underneath the Ballochmyle Railway Viaduct, a masterpiece of engineering and a designated National Historic Civil Engineering Landmark which possesses the world's largest masonry arch (181 ft) and which is still in use – a rare example of a heritage structure built right the first time and still able to be adapted and utilised.

Ayrshire's valleys conceal an interesting human history too. William Wallace hid from English troops along the trail at a viewpoint above the river now called Wallace's Seat, while the Ayrshire scenery helped inspire the poems of Robert Burns, who was born in Alloway in Ayrshire in 1759 and who bade a sad farewell (in Ayr Gorge) to his darling Highland Mary, in 1786.

The path contains a lovely assortment of all the things one expects on a river walk. There are footbridges and stepping stones, perilous-looking suspension bridges and the sturdy early 18th-century sandstone bridge at Sorn. The path tends to bypass cliffs and ridges rather than climb them, and always there is the river, that constant companion, always showing the way. There's no need for topographic maps and compasses here. Entering Ayr at the end of your walk you make your way towards Ayr Harbour and to the lighthouse at the end of South Pier – where you now have the choice of setting off either to the north or to the south on the fabulous 147-km-long Ayrshire Coastal Path which runs almost in its entirety along either sandy or rock-strewn beaches of this lovely Scottish county.

36. OFFA'S DYKE PATH
Wales and England

Distance: 285 km
Grade: Moderate to Strenuous
Time: 2 weeks

Offa's Dyke, the famous 8th-century earthwork created under the reign of the Anglian Offa, King of Mercia from 757 to 796 CE, was originally 20 m wide and up to 8 m high, measuring from the top of its wall to the bottom of its accompanying ditch. Though its precise purpose is still debated (and of late even the time frame of its construction is being argued in some scholastic circles), it appears at best to have been built to create a political and cultural boundary, and at worst as a military application in the form of a defensive wall raised to defend Mercia to the east from the Welsh 'petty kingdom' of Powys to the west. The ditch which parallels the wall on the western or Welsh side of the wall, the soil from which was used to create the embankment on the eastern Mercian side, is certainly a defensive obstacle (though a section in south Shropshire has an *eastern* ditch). However an absence of roads, fortifications, and other associated military infrastructure suggests it fell short of being a fortified frontier along the lines of a Hadrian's Wall. Whatever its true intentions, the fact is it is wholly unique, and remains as a testimony to the lost culture of the Anglian/Mercian people.

Well preserved for much of its length it runs from the banks of the Severn Estuary on the Irish Sea and ends at the Sedbury Cliffs, a boundary tangible enough to be followed with the naked eye – and tangible enough to have one of Great Britain's best-known trails run beside it. Offa's Dyke Path, opened in 1971, passes through eight counties, crosses the English/Welsh border on more than twenty occasions, and is a conduit joining three Areas of Outstanding Natural Beauty – the Clwydian Range/Dee Valley, the Shropshire Hills and the Wye Valley – as well as the Clun Forest, Brecon Beacons, the Vale of Clwyd and the Black Mountains.

Walking the trail south to north remains the preferred option, if only to have prevailing winds at your back. Starting out from Sedbury the trail passes through woodlands to the east of the Wye with a small climb of around 180 m to the Devil's Pulpit with its view to Tintern Abbey below. Also worth admiring is the lovely white Round House, a folly-like tower built in 1794 with its crenellated roof (from the top of which it was claimed you could look into nine counties) on the slopes of the Kymin to the east of Monmouth.

Monmouth to Pandy – through orchards and following lines of dry stone walls – can be a muddy walk if it's been raining, but the trail dries out from Pandy as you cross the walk's highest section along a somewhat sinuous ridgeline along the Black Mountains on a flagstone path, followed by a 677-m descent to the Welsh market town of Hay-on-Wye, in the far northeast of Brecon Beacons National Park. Laneways and farmlands take you to Newchurch and Gladestry, the local churches of which have erected welcome signs for Offa's Dyke walkers and offer milk, tea, coffee and biscuits – a sanctuary and a blessing on a rainy day. A wide grassy

Photo: Sillesoeren

path leads from Gladestry up over Hergest Ridge, a sheep-grazing moorland area over an elongated hill that straddles the Welsh/English border, and from there to Kington you'll find yourself walking along a series of sealed roads, though this may come as a relief after hours spent the previous day slogging your way through potentially muddy fields. And there's the option of stopping by the Kington Golf Club, England's highest golf course. Three peaks are bagged between Kington and Knighton – representing a cumulative elevation gain of 760 m. Don't underestimate the capacity of this trail to exhaust the novice hiker.

A series of switchbacks is next, including steep climbs and descents as well as a section on Llanfair Hill where you are actually walking upon the dyke itself. Your arrival at Brompton Crossroads will be eagerly anticipated too, especially if you've booked ahead and secured a night's accommodation in The Drewin B&B with its panoramic views over the Welsh borderlands. The walk's flattest section, from Buttington to Llanymynech, is next, and you stay on Offa's Dyke Path through the centre of Trefonen, the 'village of ash trees' where the path runs adjacent to Chapel Lane through the very heart of town.

A steep climb out of Trefonen leads through more woodlands before passing the Oswestry Old Racecourse, set in a lovely habitat of scrub, heathland, woodlands, ponds and grasslands and which saw its first horse race in the 17th century. Chirk Castle soon follows, built in 1295 and continually inhabited since 1310, with its beautiful clipped yew hedges, herbaceous borders and terraces. The Llangollen Canal is another highlight, linking Denbighshire in North Wales with Hurleston in south Cheshire and a section of which was declared a World Heritage Site in 2009. Crossing its famous 307-metre-long Pontcysyllte Aqueduct, built by Thomas Telford from 1795 to 1805 with its eighteen piers of local stone and capped with an iron trough to carry the water from its source at Horseshoe Falls, is an encounter to remember (though an alternative ground trail exists for anyone who prefers not to cross it), as is Castell Dinas Bran, the medieval castle above Llangollen and one of many hill forts in the region.

A lovely section passes along the base of the Llangollen escarpment before a steep climb on to moorlands ends in a descent to Llandegla in the upper valley of the River Alyn. A series of hilltops are then skirted on the way to Bodfari, and a last push through farmlands and hedgerows before dipping your boots in the Irish Sea and so officially completing the only one of twelve designated National Trails to follow, as closely as is possible, this extraordinary man-made feature, and Britain's longest ancient monument.

35. CAUSEWAY COAST WAY
Antrim, Northern Ireland

Distance: 51 km
Grade: Easy
Time: 2–3 days

The Antrim coast is Northern Ireland's most celebrated coastline, and the Causeway Coast Way that links the towns of Ballycastle and Portstewart passes by some of the country's most famous landmarks that make up the Giant's Causeway, the 16th-century roofless ruins of Dunluce Castle sitting

alone on its basalt promontory on the site of an earlier Irish fort, and the Carrick-a-Rede Rope Bridge.

Twenty metres long and swinging 30 m above rocks linking the tiny island of Carrick-a-Rede, once used by salmon fishermen but now existing largely as a tourist attraction and crossed by around 250,000 people a year. The trail, which is broken into six half-day sections, makes use of promenades, beaches, fabulous cliffside trails, and some roadside walking.

Walking the trail east to west has you setting out from the centre of Ballycastle to the coast, with its views out to Scotland's Mull of Kintyre from the main Coast Road (take care, there are no footpaths on this section). After a kilometre on this road take a detour from the trail to Kinbane Head, where you can walk across a dramatic limestone promontory to Kinbane Castle, built in 1547 and besieged by the English in 1551. Back on the Coast Road this is followed, with a detour or two through fields and along clifftops, through Portaneevy and along the cliff of Boheeshane Bay down to Ballintoy Harbour. Passing through the tiny hamlet of Portbradden the shoreline begins to exhibit Ice Age characteristics with its sea stacks and raised beaches, while in White Park Bay the trail passes through a hole in a sea arch at Gid Point as you make your way to Dunseverick Harbour and its jewel – the gorgeous ruins of Dunseverick Castle on a site visited by St Patrick in the 5th century, attacked by Vikings in the 9th century, and finally destroyed by Cromwellian troops in the 1650s.

The trail from Dunseverick Castle to the Giant's Causeway is the walk's longest off-road section, an isolated ramble along grassy paths around a series of impressive headlands with more sea stacks and views out to rugged, isolated Rathlin Island, former place of refuge for Robert the Bruce (in 1306), Northern Island's only inhabited offshore island,

and just a short ferry ride away if you want to punctuate your walk with a visit to its picturesque harbour and its community of 70 people.

The highest point on the Causeway Coast Way is reached at Bengore Head (100 m above sea level), and from here a series of interesting landforms seem to draw you on; appetisers on the way to the main course. There is Benbane Head, Northern Ireland's northernmost mainland point, soon after which you pass into the UNESCO World Heritage Site associated with the Giant's Causeway, though its famous amphitheatre still remains hidden from view. There is the barely discernible offshore rock formation 'Nurse and Child' in Horse Shoe Harbour, and once you get beyond Benanouran Head the first tantalising hints of what is to come suddenly appear – the isolated, free-standing columns at the head of the valley – the so-called 'Chimney Tops' which you first see from above before beginning your descent, initially via a set of stairs and then on a zig-zag path, to the amphitheatre.

A sea of interlocking basalt columns – more than 40,000 of them – the Giant's Causeway came to international attention in 1693 with the publication of a Royal Society paper by Richard Bulkeley of Trinity College in Dublin, though its existence was well known of course to locals who preferred the story that it was constructed by the Irish giant Fionn mac Cumhaill, who built it so he and the Scottish giant Benandonner could meet in the middle of the North Channel and do battle – a more dramatic explanation, surely, than volcanism, basalt intrusions, cooling and fracturing of what was left of the ancient Thulean Plateau?

The Causeway Coast Area of Outstanding Natural Beauty, established in 1989, is a 29-km stretch of the trail that includes the Giant's Causeway and the Carrick-a-Rede bridge and is particularly scenic with a rare mix of dramatic headlands, vertical and stepped cliffs, sandy beaches backed by extensive dune systems, black volcanic rocks and white chalk, as well as numerous historic landmarks and a rich diversity of flora and fauna. It is a coastline laced by other trails, too. The Causeway Coast Way is bookended by the Moyle Way and the North Sperrins Way, and the trail itself is part of the Ulster Way, a series of trails that encircle the province of Ulster.

Continuing on past Port Granny there are two options to Portballintrae – the less scenic though more direct route follows a train line to the Bush River, but the more dramatic is, of course, the clifftop trail, an identifiable path that follows the cliffs and allows for some final views back to the causeway as you make for Leckilroy Cove. A set of stairs then takes you up Runkerry Point before a descent to the shoreline and on to the pristine beauty of Runkerry Strand, an 800-metre-long beach, and the gob-smackingly ornate Runkerry House above you on the left. Footbridges and gangways are crossed on the approach to Portballintrae, and from there you head inland past a housing estate before crossing the Coast Road near Dunluce Castle, a must-do detour to one of Northern Ireland's most impressive medieval monuments. And then you reach Portrush, with its charming Port Path that takes you past idyllic coves such as Devil's Port, Holywell Port and Stoney Port, on into the town of Portstewart, and along a pedestrian path beneath O'Hara's Castle, a Dominican convent built in 1834. Finally you make your way up past St Patrick's Well on the Strand Road, where you have the option of continuing along the Ulster Way – or just walk back into Portstewart on the promenade, to begin a lifetime of reminiscing.

34. AONACH EAGACH RIDGE WALK
Glen Coe, Scotland

Distance: 9.5 km
Grade: Strenuous
Time: 6–9 hours

There is hardly a line of crags anywhere in Great Britain quite like this one, a linear ridge high above the northerly side of Glen Coe and a Grade 2 rock scramble that ticks boxes you maybe don't even want ticked – exposure, views, and adrenalin-inducing heights with goat-like trails. At times walking it is akin to threading the eye of a needle or being on a tightrope, so little room is there for error. There are just two ways off it, too, when the going is at its toughest – one at the beginning, and the other at the end. There's no deciding half-way through that you're suddenly not up to it, or thinking 'Well I've had enough of this', and absconding. And as if its knife-edge pinnacles weren't enough, add to that the vagaries of the Scottish weather, and, well …

There are a lot of stories in the scrambling community about the Aonach Eagach. People who have done it in winter are happy to admit it is dangerous, hard, even scary. If you come here you'll need a head for heights. Ropes are a grey area. Unnecessary for Grade 1 scrambling but a must-have for Grade 3s, the Grade 2 classification for the Aonach Eagach means it occupies a hazy middle-ground. Most do however prefer to pack a rope or two because rain can instantly turn the trail into something resembling a greasy ladder, not a pleasant thought when you're passing by a 900-m drop. If travelling in a group, it's a good idea to have someone who

Photo: Graham Lewis

is proficient with ropes. The trail is long and exposed, and if you've not had prior scrambling experience prior to setting out, you'd be well advised to get some.

Your ascent begins on a track 1 km southeast of Glencoe village, over a burn and along a rising slope up Am Bodach before emerging on to a *bealach* (narrow mountain pass) then making a left turn on to the ridge, which climbs steeply to Am Bodach's summit. Descending from the summit can be tricky if you're not accustomed to downclimbing (for some this can be the 'worst' part of the entire traverse) as you make your way down a steep and somewhat awkward cliff on to the ridge and towards Meall Dearg (953 m), the day's first Munro, and a view that is guaranteed to render anyone sober.

Once you arrive at Meall Dearg you see what is before you – a series of rock chimneys and a whole series of scrambling sections that are narrow, yes, though not perhaps as narrow as popular myths might have you believe. Nevertheless these are the 'Crazy Pinnacles' – a series of vertical goblin-like spires and spikes with grassy slopes plunging away on their northern and southern sides, spires that are best approached head-on rather than trying to go around them. The Crazy Pinnacles give the ridge its reputation and extend all the way to Stob Coire Leith, which is reached after a short, steep descent. With the trauma of the pinnacles now behind you, you can relax on a broad trail as you make your way towards Sgorr nam Fiannaidh (967 m), the second Munro with its wonderful views down over Glen Coe.

There are three possible routes down from Stob Coire Leith – along the rim of Clachaig Gully, though this is an eroded path that has led to several fatalities over the years; or southwards to Loch Achtriochtan, though this also is a steep descent with an abundance of scree and is best avoided.

The best choice is to turn westwards and continue towards Clachaig Gully, only stay on the ridge along a small ascent before reaching two small cairns where you turn to the right then descend on to a boggy path that zig-zags down from the Pap of Glencoe, the distinctive rounded summit above Loch Leven, itself worth walking to for the great views down Loch Leven to Kinlochleven. Stay on the path until it links up with a road that runs parallel to the A82. From there it's only a 2-km walk to the Clachaig Inn, a source of hospitality to weary travellers for over 300 years with its staples of venison, prime Scotch beef and Scottish salmon – plus more than 200 varieties of malt whisky, guaranteed to further embellish even the most harrowing of Aonach Eagach tales.

33. CAMINO DE SANTIAGO (THE WAY OF ST JAMES)
Spain and France

Distance: 800 km
Grade: Easy to Moderate
Time: 30–35 days

The Camino de Santiago is the name given to the many pilgrimage routes from England, France, Italy and elsewhere that all have as their common goal the shrine of St James, the patron saint of Spain, in the Cathedral of Santiago de Compostela in Galicia on the Iberian Peninsula. James, the son of Zebedee and Salome, was one of Jesus' twelve apostles, and one of the first to follow him. Tradition says that after the resurrection James travelled to Spain where he preached tirelessly, before seeing a vision of the Virgin Mary which

CAMINO DE SANTIAGO (THE WAY OF ST JAMES)

Photo: José Antonio Gil Martínez

Photo: Sebbe xy

prompted his return to the Holy Land. His beheading in Judea in the year 44 CE on the orders of King Herod Agrippa is the only recorded instance of the death of an apostle in the New Testament (ACTS 12: 1–2), making him very likely the first of the apostles to be martyred for his faith. His remains, it is claimed, were then taken by boat from Jerusalem back to Santiago de Compostela, where the cathedral of Santiago was built between 1075 and 1211 over the agreed site of the apostle's remains.

The trail is Europe's most ancient pilgrimage route, with the first recorded journeys dating to the 9th century. It has survived the Dark Ages, Black Plagues and Protestant reformations to become the most popular pilgrimage trail of the medieval period, and the Galician scallop shell – with its many indented lines all coming together at its centre – was then, and remains now, a symbol of the many pathways along which people converge upon this cherished place. And while the many religious houses that once were sprinkled along its route to welcome travellers are now a little harder to find, walkers and pilgrims have little trouble finding more conventional accommodation on a trail that was always designed to pass through towns and villages rather than avoid them for the sake of tranquillity, like so many other long distance paths. On the Way of St James, providing comfort and food for weary, hungry pilgrims was always good business.

And nowadays, even better business. More than 200,000 people walk these ancient trails every year, numbers greater than any ancient pilgrim could have ever dreamt possible, passing over the same rivers and hills and through the same villages that believers did a thousand years ago. There has been a boom in numbers over the past fifteen years, but gone are the days when farmers would ask pilgrims to enter their houses and share a meal and ask for little in return. Spain's economic realities have instead led to a huge growth in the number of satellite television-equipped guesthouses that cater for what some disparagingly call 'phony pilgrims', those who arrange for their luggage to be 'driven ahead' to their next hotel, who choose not to seek out the basic three-course 'pilgrims' meals', or stay in sleeping bag-filled hostel halls with a hundred other wayfarers. Times have changed.

The most popular route without doubt is the Camino Frances, the 'French Way', which begins in St Jean-Pied-du-Port on the French side of the Pyrenees and crosses the border into the small Spanish village of Roncesvalles on the Urrobi River, famous as the site of the defeat of Charlemagne in 778 CE. From Roncesvalles it is a further 780 km to Santiago de Compostela via Pamplona, Logrono, Burgos, Leon and beautiful Ponferrada, surrounded by mountains on the Sil River and the last major city before your destination. (Don't leave without visiting its magnificent 12th-century Templar Castle.)

In terms of landscape, the Camino de Santiago lacks for nothing. The alpine vistas of the Pyrenees, the treeless and windswept Meseta Plateau, the green fertile mountains of Galicia the 'country of a thousand rivers', and finally the rugged Atlantic coast. If you decide you want to avoid the crowds and do it from November to April, the trail will be less crowded but shorter days due to fog, rain and the like will result in shorter sections walked and therefore more overnight stays, raising the cost. The pilgrim-like, solitary experience you will have, however, will likely more than compensate if that is what you're looking for.

The Camino Frances is the most developed of all the Camino routes, has the most extensive trail markers, and a never-ending choice of hostels, guesthouses and hotels.

Walking it will take you through seven provinces and a wealth of human history that is just too numbing to attempt to describe here. Rest days along its 33 stages can be taken in towns such as Pamplona (don't walk all day, it's a 'rest day'!), and if you take the time to get to know some of your fellow walkers representing 130 nations then chances are you'll barely notice you've just walked alongside 90 km of paved roads, 203 km of streets through sleepy villages, and 505 km of ancient, story-laden trails.

32. CHANNEL ISLAND WAY
Channel Islands, England

Distance: 185 km
Grade: Easy to Moderate
Time: 14 days

Internally self-governing territories of the British crown and known collectively as the 'Channel Islands', the five largest islands in this charming archipelago – Jersey, Guernsey, Alderney, Sark and Herm – are now linked by the Channel Islands Way which opened in the spring of 2011 after five years spent piecing together its 185-km segmented route on Jersey (77 km), Guernsey (61 km), Alderney (22 km), Sark (15 km), and Herm (10.5 km). The ferry connections required to complete the trail are straightforward enough, thanks to efficient and long-established inter-island links, and the larger islands' segments have been limited to between 3 and 6.5 km in length and include bus stops, pubs, cafes and restaurants – infrastructure that should ease any logistical, or island-hopping, concerns. Jersey and Guernsey are less than an hour's ferry ride apart, there are several hour-long services a week to Sark from Jersey and Guernsey from April to September, and Alderney and Herm are a short hop from Guernsey.

This almost seamless series of island trails, a five-course feast if you like, of sandy beaches, rocky promontories and secluded bays, ranges from walks through large urban centres such as St Helier on Jersey to quiet strolls on tiny Herm, the smallest and least-populated island with only a scattering of buildings at its centre and a few kilometres of sandy roads. Alderney's coastal path passes over dramatic clifftops and encircles almost the entire island, which has a lovely community feel to it, while Sark, which lies just 13 km off the Normandy Coast, has its own unique blend of French cultural influences.

The walk brings together the Channel Islands' very best coastal and inland trails. On Jersey you can walk from Rozel Bay to Bouley Bay on its wild and less populated northeast coast, and take a 13.5-km south coast trail around St Aubin and the beautiful arc of St Brelade's Bay that will include some Second World War German bunkers if you continue walking to nearby Noirmont Point. On Guernsey a path above the island's capital of St Peter Port takes you into Bluebell Woods which every April transform into a gorgeous carpet of blue, and no matter where you walk on Guernsey you are never far away from one of the island's fifteen loophole towers, built by the British from 1778 to 1779 to defend Guernsey against French incursions. Made of Guernsey granite the towers are of a common design – all are circular with three floors – and provide an ideal series of well-placed markers as you make your way around the island.

Photo: G.Mannaerts

Alderney has over 80 km of laneways and walking paths on an island that measures just 5 km by 3 km at its widest point. Continuously inhabited for over 5,000 years, the island's west coast and the area out to the northern gannet colony on Burhou Island are a designated Ramsarsite (wetlands of international importance), but it is Alderney's beaches that are its star attractions – Saye Beach and Braye Bay, rockpool-encrusted Longis Bay, and the sheltered northern beach of Arch Bay. Just don't leave the island without visiting the Nunnery, Britain's best-preserved small Roman fort, and if you have the time you can head 'inland' and walk the 5-km-long Les Rochers Trail, a path that begins at the Visitor's Centre in St Anne and goes along its quaint Main Street and on to a grass track then past an *Abreuvoir Publique*, old cattle troughs still common to the island. In its less-visited interior there are stands of sycamore and ash, entrances to Second World War German tunnel networks, and the 43 acres of Les Rochers' native woodlands.

The walking starts the moment you get off the boat on Sark, where a trail leads to Les Laches and superb views over Creux Harbour. The trail continues past the Dew Pond, a man-made depression used for watering the island's animals, and in the few minutes it takes to get there you've already adjusted to this most esoteric of islands where the only transport permitted are horse-drawn vehicles, and bicycles (including electric bicycles for the elderly among its 600-strong population). Sark was uninhabited as recently as the 16th century, when it was used as a place of refuge for pirates, and that same sense of solitude can still be felt today.

On the smallest island of Herm the walking can get a little crowded with over 100,000 people arriving via ferry during a typical summer season, so try for a non-seasonal visit if you can, a maxim that could be applied to all of these temperate islands.

You'd probably need two weeks to walk all the trails that exist on these five outposts of Britishness off the French coast, but the beauty of the Channel Islands Way lies in its flexibility – to be able to tackle its hidden coves, craggy cliffs and sea caves one island at a time, while fulmars, cormorants and oystercatchers circle in the air above, and there are sand martins, green lizards, butterflies (over 50 species on Jersey alone – the island also supports a population of red squirrels) and orchids aplenty in the grasslands and dunes that surround you.

31. KERRY WAY
County Kerry, Ireland

Distance: 214 km
Grade: Strenuous
Time: 9 days

The Iveragh Peninsula in County Kerry is the largest peninsula in southwest Ireland. And it is also a place of legends, filled with place names like Lough Brin and Bealach Oisin that hark back to the *Fianna*, a curious mix of landless warriors and young aristocrats from Irish mythology who roamed these lands waiting for their inheritance. The peninsula also contains the tallest mountain summit in Ireland – Carrauntoohil (3,406 ft) – itself surrounded by hundreds of other peaks within the inland Macgillycuddy's

Photo: Dirtsc

Reeks mountain range, beneath the summits of which you'll come to know the beauty of this diverse peninsula in a way those in cars, driving the more-or-less parallel Ring of Kerry driving route, could never imagine.

A National Waymarked Trail, the Kerry Way is one of Ireland's most demanding walks as it takes you along a mix of old coach roads and long-abandoned pathways the Irish call *boreens* on a journey that packs an accumulated ascent over the course of its 214 km in excess of 13,000 ft. Needless to say, this is not a walk for the faint-hearted.

It begins in the popular tourist town of Killarney on the northeastern shore of Loch Leane and follows the arc of Castlelough Bay through a deciduous woodland and past 19th-century Muckross House, completed in 1843 and visited by Queen Victoria in 1861. You're now at your first 'discretionary' juncture – a 90-minute return walk to the summit of Torc Mountain, or following the Owengarriff River before climbing to Friar's Glen and your first views to distant Macgillycuddy's Reeks. Marshy areas follow, and there's a gorge walk up to Esknamucky Glen and down to Galway's Bridge. You're welcome to take a horse and cart through the Black Valley, but you'll want to walk the Gap of Dunloe, a narrow 11-km-long mountain pass between Macgillycuddy's Reeks and Purple Mountain.

A steep, rocky and often wet ascent to a saddle beneath Broaghnabinnia (2,444 ft) is followed by an equally slippery descent into the Bridia Valley. The misleadingly named Lack Road, a zig-zagging sheep's path, takes you over the next pass, and care should be taken when you step on to the narrow, sealed road into Glencar. Forests, forestry roads, primeval dells, quiet back roads and moorlands lead on to a saddle at Windy Gap and its views over neighbouring Dingle Peninsula to the north on the way to Glenbeigh, set in a horseshoe of surrounding hills and known locally as the 'Jewel in the Ring of Kerry'.

There are always things to be mindful of, both natural and man-made, on a walk like this. Wear proper hiking boots as you near Coars as the surrounding land has an extremely 'boggy' reputation, and a recent diversion now sees the trail turn left, not right, on the approach to Cahersiveen. And there are also some quite long sections with significant gaps between accommodation options, so plan these sections carefully.

The trail crosses the summit of Knockavahaun (1,217 ft) after 2.5 km of hard climbing before descending into a broad valley which puts you on a sealed road into Mastergeehy, one of the many isolated townships you encounter on the Kerry Way. The next town, Waterville, was frequently visited by Charlie Chaplin and from there you have the choice of an inland or a coastal route to Caherdaniel, where you simply must pay a visit to Staigue Stone Fort, one of Ireland's largest ring forts and finest examples of the art of dry stone walling. Leaving Staigue, ridge walking and more forest trails take you over the Kenmare and Bunnow Rivers, over *another* mountain ridge and along back roads paralleling the Owreagh River before passing through Sneem, Tahilla and Blackwater Bridge where the trail follows the estuary of the Blackwater River before passing the ruins of the 13th-century Cappanacush Castle, then through Templenoe to Kenmare. The trail climbs from Kenmare over mountain saddles on an old coach road before descending into Killarney National Park. Created in 1932 and Ireland's first national park, it contains the country's only native herd of red deer and is one of the few places in Ireland that has been continually covered in woodland since the end of the last Ice Age. Once again you enter Galway's Bridge and the trail up Cromaglan

Mountain back to Killarney, and your Kerry Way circular trail is done.

If you only have a few days to spare for the Kerry Way and want to spend them wisely, the trail's most spectacular 60-km-long section from Killarney to Glenbeigh can be done in as little as three days, or the 30 km between Sneem and Waterville is another option at under two days. And the options are indeed many. In 1982, when members of the Laune Mountaineering Club and An Taisce (the National Trust for Ireland) first suggested that a vast single trail loop could be created by linking up some of the Kerry Peninsula's sinuous, web-like paths, little did they know they were creating what one day would be acknowledged as, quite simply, Ireland's most popular walking trail.

30. SKERRIES CIRCULAR
Shetland Islands, Scotland

Distance: 9.7 km
Grade: Easy
Time: 4 hours

There's only a mile of sealed road and a population of 70–80 on the two square miles of rock and pasture that constitute Housay and Bruray, the only inhabited islands in the tiny collection of islands, islets and sea stacks that make up the all-too-easily overlooked Out Skerries. Yet with the Shetlands boasting more than 1,600 km of spectacularly rugged coastline, you're entitled to ask: why transit through those larger islands, where there are more than enough coastal walks to satisfy the most ardent of coastal addicts, to come here? The answer, though, lies very likely in the same notion that got you thinking about coming to the Shetlands in the first place – the lure of isolation – despite being well connected to the world beyond with car ferries running a daily service out of Vidlin (1.5 hours) and twice a week out of Lerwick (2.5 hours). There are also 20-minute inter-island flights available out of Tingwall Airport on Mainland.

The Out Skerries lie 14 km to the east of the main Shetland Island group, and are Scotland's most easterly landfall. The Norwegian coast, for goodness' sake, is a scant 320 km away, and so when you walk here you're combing the very fringes of Great Britain. Housay and Bruray, which have been joined to one another by a bridge since 1957, possess some of the loveliest natural harbours to be found in the Shetlands, and their rocky landscape of gneiss along their coastlines, combined with a band of internal limestone underneath grazed moorlands, exudes an overwhelming aesthetic quality. The Out Skerries' mainstay is fishing and salmon farming, and if you happen to like scuba diving there are a couple of 17th- and 18th-century Dutch East Indiamen wrecks to explore in waters that – thanks to the North Atlantic Drift – aren't quite as cold as you might think. There are three listed buildings – the Bruray Harbour Shop, the Grunay Lighthouse Keeper's House, and the Out Skerries lighthouse on Bound Skerry, Scotland's northernmost light, completed in 1858, as well as sixteen known archaeological sites including the 13-metre circle of Bronze Age boulders at Battle Pund.

The sheltered inner shorelines of the islands are home to their only communities, the houses of which hug their mile-long strip of bitumen, while beyond them the islands

Photo: Davide Gorla

are uninhabited save for sheep that graze on its thin soils. Beginning at the pier on Housay you can walk around the island and neighbouring Bruray in a few hours. The coast is rugged and windswept, with rock-strewn shorelines, tiny sounds, and cliffs broken up by gullies on an indented coastline that would likely double the length of your walk if you went to the end of every headland, though the narrow and quite beautiful headland of Mio Ness on Housay's southwest tip should definitely be walked in its entirety. A 20-minute walk up North Hill (elevation 141 ft) provides wonderful views across the water from Noss to Unst, while a walk around the north banks gives views out to the jagged sea stacks of the Hevda Skerries off Bruray Island. Along the shingle beaches at the North Mouth you'll see deposits of pale pink calcite, and inland not far from there you'll likely be able to find what islanders call the 'Old Village', an area of particularly fertile soil criss-crossed by stone dykes and the only spot in all the Skerries from which you don't have a clear line of sight to the sea. Once back at the harbour you can cross the bridge linking Housay to Bruray and make a circuit of this tiny island. Just be sure to take care around its overhanging cliffs.

As good and invigorating as the walking is here, the fact is many come not for the walking, but for the wildlife. If you want to share a cliff edge with a colony of puffins just a metre or two away, here is where you can do it. Kittiwakes, guillemots, gannets, fulmars and other sea birds are everywhere – hardly a surprising fact when you consider these islands are the first landfall west of Norway. The Shetlands are also preferable to the more southerly Orkneys if you're wanting to see peregrines, short-eared owls and other birds of prey, as well as whooper swans, pink-footed geese, and whales.

The population might now only be half what it was in the mid-1800s, but its residents are a hardy bunch, always ready with a warm welcome and always willing to share the island's stories – from its beginnings as a Norse settlement to its increasingly bright future as a tourism destination with establishments like the Rocklea Crofthouse on Bruray, a registered croft set on nine acres and providing respite to those who like to walk on the fringes of our world and who favour mottos like: 'If you're not on the edge, you're taking up too much space'.

29. GREAT STONES WAY
Wiltshire, England

Distance: 58 km (excluding optional trails)
Grade: Easy
Time: 3 days

To walk the Great Stones Way through the tranquil, rolling downs and chalk grasslands of Wiltshire is to walk through the Neolithic prehistory of England. For more than a millennium from 3,000 BCE to 2,000 BCE these fields were the scene of frenzied activity as henges, burial mounds and processional avenues were built to provide pathways to the afterlife and to help those who constructed them come to an understanding of the world in which they lived.

The trail owes its existence to the Friends of the Ridgeway, supporters of that ancient trail from Salisbury Plain to East Anglia considered by many to be Britain's oldest road, who are keen to develop a single walking trail extending

Photo: Geotrekker72

across southern England and whose efforts led to the trail's opening in 2014.

The trail begins outside Swindon at Barbury Castle, an Iron Age hill fort first occupied 2,500 years ago with two defensive ditches and ramparts, and made use of during the Roman occupation because of the extensive views it provides – on a clear day – from the Cotswolds to the River Severn. The trail passes through the heart of the fort and continues on a broad track to Hackpen Hill from which a small detour takes you to the Winterbourne Bassett White Horse, one of Wiltshire's famous chalk horses, this one cut in 1838 to commemorate the coronation of Queen Victoria. You now descend to Overton Hill, and through the Fyfield Down National Nature Reserve with its scattering of ancient sarsen stones used to construct the stone circles at Avebury, the three sets of which you'll soon begin to see ahead of you and which includes the largest stone circle of its kind in Europe. You can either return to the trail the way you came, or better is to head south to see the prehistoric artificial chalk mound at Silbury Hill (part of the Stonehenge, Avebury and Associated Sites UNESCO World Heritage Site) which, at 98 ft in height, is Europe's tallest prehistoric man-made mound, before crossing the River Kennet and rejoining the trail at East Kennet. Also be sure to walk over to West Kennet and see the West Kennet Long Barrow, constructed around 3,600 BCE, 400 years before Stonehenge, and have a look inside its accessible (though empty) chambered tomb, while nearby is The Sanctuary. Originally an arrangement of circular wooden posts, the unearthing of several human skeletons suggests the site had a ritualistic function.

A small ascent up Lurkeley Hill leads to the Wansdyke, a series of medieval defensive earthworks comprising a ditch and running embankment and the remains of the old Roman-built London to Bath road. Descend to the Lockeridge–Alton Barnes road and take an allowed path through a field to Walkers Hill and the Neolithic Adam's Grave, a destroyed Neolithic long barrow. Pass through the villages of Alton Priors and Alton Barnes, with views out over the wonderfully undulating fields of the Vale of Pewsey, and make for the towpath of the Kennet and Avon Canal at Honeystreet, built between 1794 and 1810 and linking the Kennet and Avon rivers. Continue on the towpath for a serene 1.5 km then turn right towards Woodborough which takes you on a bridleway (and a few roads, though with little traffic and lovely views) before another bridleway leads to Combe Cottage and up on to the edge of Salisbury Plain. From here you have a fine view back to the Alton Barnes White Horse before following the edge of the plateau on to Casterley Camp, the site of a Romano-British enclosure with a single circuit of ramparts.

Walk along through open grassland past Field Barn towards the Ministry of Defence site at West Chisenbury Farm and along another grassy path past Compton Farm towards the A345. Cross the Avon at Coombe, enter the hamlet of Fifield, then pass a series of artificial lakes leading into the village of Netheravon. Stroll down its delightful High Street, and where the road forks, head left and over the Avon again to Choulston Farm.

Descending to the River Avon the trail passes through more villages before offering another optional loop, this time to Durrington Walls, a large Neolithic settlement which scholars suggest may have been for a brief period the largest settlement in northern Europe, and which very likely doubled as a 'builder's camp' during the construction of Stonehenge. Close to Durrington Walls is Woodhenge, a timber circle first identified in 1925, containing 168 post holes (now marked with contemporary concrete posts) in six concentric oval rings. The timber posts that once stood here were likely free-standing, weighed up to five tons each, and are thought to have supported a ring-shaped building used for ceremonial and religious purposes.

You then walk along Stonehenge Avenue, part of the original route used to transport the dead to their final resting places at Stonehenge, one of the world's most famous prehistoric monuments with its evocative remains of standing stones located at the centre of England's largest concentration of Neolithic and Bronze Age relics. The final stage of the trail leads to the impressive Iron Age fort at Old Sarum, later added to by the Normans who built a town – the remains of which have only recently been rediscovered – buried beneath the ground behind its massive earthwork defences.

Despite being created to highlight Wiltshire's monuments, there is far more than just man-made history here. These grasslands support an abundance of flowering plants, butterflies and birdlife, including – if one is lucky – a sighting of the Great Bustard, the male of which is possibly the heaviest flying animal on earth. On Salisbury Plain you'll find the burnt-tip orchid and the endangered mining bee, and everywhere you look there are 'chalk downland specialists' such as clustered bellflowers, and the purplish bells of autumn gentians.

Nowhere in England, however, does a trail pack so much history into such a short trail, and if you want to add a little 'contemporary' history to the trail you can carry on into Salisbury and end your walk at magnificent Salisbury Cathedral, the foundation stone of which was laid on 28 April 1220 – a bit of a latecomer, really, in this ancient and revered landscape.

28. DALES WAY
West Yorkshire and Cumbria, England

Distance: 135 km
Grade: Easy
Time: 6–8 days

It has been described as 'Britain's gentlest long distance path'. Tracing a southeast/northwest line through the Yorkshire and Cumbrian countryside, the Dales Way is a long distance footpath carved out of the landscape by volunteers in 1991. It requires neither the amount of time nor the stamina to complete that is needed of other long distance footpaths such as the Pennine Way and the Coast to Coast, and so makes a more agreeable introduction to multi-day hikes for the novice walker. Taking advantage of river valleys the elevation gain/loss is minimal, and it can be completed in as little as four days, although the fact that virtually every pub you pass – and there are many – also has rooms, means you might want to factor in a couple of well-earned 'rest days'.

The Dales Way runs from Ilkley in West Yorkshire to Bowness-on-Windermere in Cumbria, paralleling river banks wherever possible. It is a trail of two halves: the first takes you upstream along the River Wharfe through Wharfedale, considered by many to be the prettiest of all the Yorkshire Dales, and on through the Yorkshire Dales National Park then over the roof of England on the Pennine watershed at Ribblehead; the second half takes you through a series of river valleys – the Dentdale, the Mint and the Kent – and ends surrounded by the beauty of the Lake District on the shores of Lake Windermere.

Photo: Mtaylor848

Photo: John S Turner

Starting at Ilkley you walk through the scenery of Lower Wharfedale to the day's unquestioned highlight – the Augustinian priory of Bolton Abbey. Founded in 1154 on the banks of the River Wharfe it still had not been completed four centuries later when the Dissolution of the Monasteries brought an end to religious life at the priory in 1540. From the abbey you then enter one of Britain's most tranquil stretches of woodland riverside walking along the Strid, a remarkable section of the River Wharfe that narrows to only 60 cm in width, though what it lacks in width it makes up for in depth as it becomes a rushing 'vertical' torrent that has undercut its banks and is extremely dangerous.

From Burnsall to Hubberholme the trail runs mostly on the valley floor, except for a section of high ground at the half-way point that takes you up on to an impressive expanse of limestone paving, the so-called 'grykes' – individual slabs called 'clints' each separated from the other by vertical gaps up to a metre deep. Leaving Hubberholme a section of dark, peaty hollows can make the going tough as you climb to the highest point on the trail over bleak, open moorlands. Keep in mind there are no shops on the coming 37-km section between Buckden and Dent village.

The next day you follow the River Dee into the picturesque valley of Dentdale and then on to the even more charming village of Dent, the valley's only village full of whitewashed cottages and cobblestoned streets. Leaving Dent the trail tenaciously hugs a series of riverbanks as you begin to leave behind all of those typically 'Dales' landscapes before arriving in Sedbergh, with its lovely views out over the Howgill Fells, one of England's 'forgotten' walking areas with its domed fells once described by acclaimed fell-walker Alfred Wainwright as 'looking like a herd of sleeping elephants'. A day's walking will then take you into Burneside, and from there it's just a half-day's walk to the end of the trail at Bowness-on-Windermere.

The trail is never far away from points of man-made interest that include Roman roads, manor houses and suspension bridges, and because of its modest elevation is a doable walk in spring and autumn. Nicely waymarked and easy on the feet, the Dales Way is a perfect introduction to the joys of the long distance footpath.

27. WALES COAST PATH
Monmouthshire to Flintshire, Wales

Distance: 1,400 km
Grade: Moderate
Time: 3 months

It's a rare thing for a walker to say they've traced the outline of a nation, the term some give to a successful completion of the Wales Coast Path which follows the entirety of the Welsh coast as best it can from Queensferry in the north to Chepstow in the south. And while even a cursory acquaintance with Welsh geography makes it pretty clear you've fallen short of circumnavigating all of it if you've left out Offa's Dyke Path and the entire Welsh/English border, well, one should not quibble. Offa's Dyke Path – which connects to the coastal path anyway, thus making a true circumnavigation possible for those with too much time on their hands – is a mere 285 km in length; a stroll in comparison to the 1,408 km that comprises this epic trail.

Conceived in the wake of the commercial benefits and

Photo: Chembeth

growth in tourism the popular Pembrokeshire Coast Path and the Isle of Anglesey Coastal Path have brought to their local economies, the various segments of this remarkable path, created over seven years from 2007 to 2014 (though officially opened on 5 May 2012), welcomed 2.8 million walkers in its first year. It is broken up into eight geographical areas, which from north to south are: North Wales Coast and Dee Estuary; the Isle of Anglesey; Menai, Llyn and Meirionnydd; Ceredigion; Pembrokeshire; Carmarthenshire; Gower and Swansea Bay; and the South Wales Coast and the Severn Estuary.

As the first dedicated continuous walking route in the world to be as physically and legally close to its coastline as it was possible to get, its creators have devised a path that is an amalgam of existing trails and a series of new 'connector' trails, and is a clarion call to all lovers of wildlife. Encompassing eleven National Nature Reserves and dozens of Sites of Special Scientific Interest, the path passes through the Dee Estuary, Wales's largest estuary and home to over 100,000 wintering birds; and past Wales's only little tern breeding colony in the Gronant Dunes near Prestatyn, which are themselves the only unmodified remnant of far larger systems of dunes remaining on the North Wales coast. There have been sightings of snow buntings – the high Arctic songbird – along the regenerated sea front at Rhyl in Denbighshire, and the heath habitat on the limestone headland that is the Great Orme has a population of the silver-studded blue butterfly, a species under threat elsewhere in the UK but thriving here. The Precambrian cliffs near Holyhead off the west coast of Anglesey Island contain large colonies of guillemots and razorbills, Cemlyn Bay has Arctic and sandwich terns, Newborough Warren has one of the UK's largest raven colonies, and there are the hanging oak woodlands at Penderi Cliffs near Llanrhystud – sessile oaks whose normally tall stature has been stunted by persistent sea winds.

Naturally the trail bisects the Pembrokeshire Coast National Park, the only coastal park in Britain, where you'll see the fresh and saltwater marshes of Carmarthenshire backed by pine forests and sand dunes, and the remarkable coastline of the Gower Peninsula, the UK's very first designated Area of Outstanding Natural Beauty. In the south you'll walk the 22 km of the Glamorgan Heritage Coast with its multitude of soaring sandstone cliffs between Ogmore and Rhoose Point, and the mud flats along the Severn that lead you to the Norman remains of Chepstow Castle above the River Wye, Britain's oldest surviving post-Roman stone fort.

Along the way you'll visit a series of man-made and cultural points of interest too, such as the Neolithic burial chamber not far from Lligway, Edward I's Conwy Castle with its wonderfully preserved 800-year-old medieval walls, Caernarfon Castle, the most expensive castle ever built by an English king, and all along the trail a smattering of 6th-century Celtic churches. You will walk along Cei Bach, the beach near which Dylan Thomas lived and wrote, and on the Llyn Peninsula you can take a well-deserved break and catch the ferry to Bardsley Island, the 'Island of 20,000 Saints' which, if visited three times, is considered the spiritual equivalent of a religious pilgrimage to Rome. On the Llyn Peninsula there's the birthplace of T. E. Lawrence ('Lawrence of Arabia') in Tremadoc, and of David Lloyd George at Llanystumdwy. There are, of course, more 'earthy' establishments as well – such as Ye Olde Bulls Head Inn in Beaumaris on Anglesey Island with its low ceilings and wall displays of antique weaponry, where Charles Dickens helped himself to a glass of ale during a stay in 1859.

In the end, though, it will be the unspoilt beaches – the best in Britain – that will leave the deepest impression. The sand dunes of the Dee Estuary, the sheltered coves of Gwynedd, Ceredigion's 'giant's tooth' rock of Carreg Bica on Llangrannog Beach, and the dozens of award-winning beaches along the Pembrokeshire coast.

And if you have an interest in maritime history, no matter how obscure or niche, the good news is that – at some point – you're bound to be passing by where it all happened. Cardigan, the great 16th-century shipbuilding hub, is where emigrants departed to the new worlds of the United States, Canada and Australia when the harvest failed in 1816. There are still faint echoes of the glory days of the trawlers and drifters that made up the Milford Haven and Tenby fishing fleets. Whatever your maritime fancy might be, you'll find it here on Britain's longest waymarked trail.

26. CAPE WRATH TRAIL
Highland, Scotland

Distance: 312–357 km
Grade: Strenuous
Time: 12–21 days

If you're the pioneering type who aches for a challenge, who has no qualms about backpacking for days over mountainous terrain, who prefers not to walk on 'established' trails where only a single option presents itself as a way forward, you need to consider coming here. If you like traversing landscapes that are oddly familiar while passing through remote glens and nameless bogs that will test the boundaries of your endurance, on a trail that pulls you forward because you've done your research and know the splendours that await you at journey's end, then it's likely Scotland's Cape Wrath Trail is the walk you've been looking for.

It follows drovers' routes and old funeral paths (corpse roads) once marked by coffin stones, all trampled into existence by crofters herding cattle through the rugged highlands, and by communities whose loved ones had died but because they lived in villages without churches had to be taken for miles to receive proper burials. There is a basic template to follow here, of course, despite the trail not being waymarked, thanks in no small part to the publication in 1996 of *The Cape Wrath Trail* by David Paterson. He began at the trail's accepted starting point at Fort William and made his way north to Glenfinnan and on to the challenging terrain of Knoydart, through Shiel Bridge and Strathcarron to Inverlael and through to the end of the trail at Cape Wrath. But that is only an option. The starting point may be Fort William, and the end of it the hand-dressed stones and granite blocks of the lovely Robert Stevenson-engineered 1828 lighthouse overlooking Cape Wrath – but where the 'in-between' will take you? Well, that can be a little harder to define.

With nearly 10,000 m of ascent the Cape Wrath Trail is routinely considered one of the toughest trails in Great Britain, despite having a feel of the 'theatrical' about it on Day one as you leave Fort William on the ferry to Camusnagaul. Rough going soon follows though from Glenfinnan to Glen Dessarry, and then that first taste of real wilderness as you pass Loch Hourn, northwest Scotland's most fjord-like sea loch. (You can also take an alternative route out of Fort

Photo: Graham Lewis

William following the Great Glen Way via the Caledonian Canal and Loch Linnhe before rejoining the main route at Glen Shiel.) Climbing along the Forcan Ridge you descend into Glen Shiel through one of Scotland's most spectacular mountain passes and make an overnight stop in Shiel Bridge. A nature route takes you past the Falls of Glomach, possibly Britain's loveliest waterfalls and a spectacular sight as the water tumbles over its 113-m drop.

The route then turns inland to Oykel Bridge and on to Glencoul via Ben More (1,174 m), the highest mountain in the Crianlarich Hills. Foinaven (911 m) and Arkle (787 m) are next with their wonderful landscapes of boulder-strewn fields, ridges and crags (Arkle's scree-clad slopes look daunting but in fact it is easily conquered), and then a final stretch past Rhiconich to the far northwest coast. Here you cross some moorlands as you make your way to Sandwood Bay, largely uninhabited since 1847 when the area was cleared for sheep grazing, and at last comes the welcoming sight of Cape Wrath lighthouse.

If planned carefully, a traverse of the Cape Wrath Trail can be done staying in a mix of hotels, B&Bs and bothies – ruined buildings restored to a primitive standard that can range in size from box-like spaces the size of a small shed to larger stone cottages. Bothies are left unlocked but have no bedding or mattresses – so be sure to bring your sleeping bag. And they can be full to bursting, too, which is why you generally don't do this trail without a tent). It may all sound a little primitive, and certainly there are fewer accommodation options than on many of Scotland's more trampled trails, but it is this trail's lack of amenities, and its quiet determination to avoid commercialisation, that contributes to its considerable – and growing – allure.

25. ULURU CIRCUIT
Northern Territory, Australia

Distance: 10.5 km
Grade: Easy
Time: 4 hours

From far away Australia's best-known natural landmark appears smooth, almost featureless, though up close it is anything but – a weathered giant covered in holes, gashes, caves, valleys and potholes. No matter how you approach it, whether you stand at a distance and watch its ephemeral colours progress through a thousand hues at sunrise or sunset, whether you seek and are given permission by the Anangu people, the rock's traditional Aboriginal owners, to make the 1.6-km climb to its summit, or whether you walk around its base and discover its mix of acacia woodlands and grassy claypans, it will be an encounter with the symbolic heart of a continent that will live long in the memory.

Uluru is in the Simpson Desert in the southern region of Australia's Northern Territory, 335 km southwest of the town of Alice Springs. It is 348 m high, and has a circumference of 9.4 km, though as massive as it is, it is like an iceberg, with most of it lying hidden beneath the surface. Geologists call it an inselberg – an isolated rock that rises abruptly from the surrounding landscape. Formed over a period spanning some 600 million years it is the world's second-largest monolith (the largest being Mount Augustus in Western Australia), its characteristic redness (its actual colour is grey) coming from the rusting of the iron in its arkose rock, a type of sandstone that's really more of a textually immature sedimentary rock.

Photo: Corey Leopold

Uluru has been sacred to the Anangu for tens of thousands of years. They believe it to have been born during *Tjukurpa*, the 'creation period', when their ancestral being made not only the Australian landscape, but the entire world. From *Tjukurpa* came everything they hold dear – traditions, religious heritage, and the ways of daily life. *Tjukurpa* provides laws on how to care for one another, and how to care for the land, and tells of the inter-relationships that exist between animals, plants, humans and the environment around them in a land that is still inhabited by the ancestors and their spirits. It's important to know something of this before arriving here. When you come to Uluru you need to understand the ancient world you are entering, both geological and ancestral, a proper appreciation of both that will greatly enhance your sense of discovery.

The Anangu would prefer if you do not walk on the rock, though as mentioned, permits are available and many people in fact do so every year. The circuit (or base walk), however, is there as the ideal compromise and in many ways will provide a far more intimate, solitary experience of Uluru than you'll get walking in a conga line to the top. The circuit is best started at either the Mala or Kuniya car parks, and is a flat, wheelchair-friendly, easy-to-follow dirt path that in places resembles snake-like grooves, which the Anangu will tell you were made by the ancestral being Kuniya as it journeyed to the nearby Mutitjulu waterhole. Trees and shrubs, including acacias, bloodwoods and native grasses, flourish in Uluru's sheltered gorges, and some twenty species of native mammals live in its shadows including black-flanked rock wallabies, the marsupial mole, the spinifex hopping mouse and malleefowl, a ground-dwelling solitary bird the size of a chicken.

In addition to walking the full circuit there are also a

number of shorter trails as well as ranger-assisted walks. The 1.5-hour, 2-km-long Mala Walk is a free ranger-led walk along the rock's northern side that begins at 8am each day from October through to April, and 10am from April to September. The ranger, a local Anangu, takes you along a shaded track, pausing to discuss points of Aboriginal law, rock art, and the history and lifestyle of his people, and it ends at the rock's lovely Kantju Gorge with its large semi-permanent waterhole beneath steep canyon walls where you'll learn about some of the dramatic creation-time events the Anangu believe were responsible for the creation of the rock. The Mutitjulu Walk is a 45-minute return, 1-km walk along Uluru's southern side that leads to a waterhole which is home to Wanampi, an ancestral watersnake.

Uluru is part of the Uluru-Kata Tjuta National Park, the 512 square miles of which also include the 36,500-million-year old conglomerate rock domes of Kata Tjuta – colloquially known as The Olgas, 25 km to the west of Uluru and set in a surprisingly lush desert landscape. The Olgas – the tallest peak of which is 200 m higher than Uluru – once had a myriad of walks but most have now been closed due to environmental and cultural considerations. The two that remain, however, make any visit here worthwhile: the 3-hour Valley of the Winds Trail, and the shorter Walpa Gorge Walk, both of which end in fine lookouts. The Olgas and Uluru, both of which are close enough to be seen from midway between the two, perfectly bookend any visit to Australia's 'Red Centre'.

24. DERWENT VALLEY HERITAGE WAY
Derbyshire, England

Distance: 88 km
Grade: Easy
Time: 6–9 days

In 1951 the Peak District – that lovely swathe of hinterland that provides a rural sanctuary for the people of neighbouring Manchester and Sheffield – became the UK's first national park after years of lobbying led to the passing of legislation in 1949 to set aside and begin to preserve the UK's areas of great natural beauty. A transitional zone with furrowed pastures, forests and limestone in the south, and crag-topped dales, coarse-grit sandstone – what climbers like to call 'God's own rock' – and the emergent slopes of the Pennine chain in the north, you might think it, then, an irony, that such a landscape could be a backdrop for a walk that has substantial leftovers of the early Industrial Age as one of its prime attractions. But the Derwent Valley has a deserved reputation for rule-breaking. It was here where large-scale industrial production was transplanted into a rural landscape for the very first time, where an employer showed that caring for the welfare of your workers is good business, and it was here where it was decided a trail that combined the best of this beautiful river valley with buildings that speak of England's grand era of industrial innovation could be combined to showcase the beauty of nature and the ingenuity of man.

The trail, which was officially opened in 2003, begins on

the shoreline of Ladybower Reservoir, the dam wall of which you cross before taking the dam's old construction rail line, crossing a bridge over the River Noe and making your way to the Derwent's riverbank at Shatton which then follows the river to Leadmill Bridge. The trail passes under a lovely green canopy of overhanging trees at Coppice Wood, continues through Chatsworth and then straightens on the approach to Rowsley to compensate for the river's meandering course. Leaving Rowsley on the A6 and crossing the river over Darley Bridge we come to Matlock, a former spa town which tumbles down its hillside like a medieval Italian village, its high point of Wellington Street an impressive 110 m above Causeway Lane. Leaving Matlock you have a choice: take a footbridge over the Derwent and follow the A6 to Matlock Bath, or for breathtaking views over Derwent Gorge take the path under the bridge and an iron arch and ascend the ridge to High Tor summit then down to Matlock Bath via the cable car station.

Leaving Matlock Bath on the River Derwent you now enter the area of the Derwent Valley Mills, a glorious mix of 18th- and 19th-century cotton mills, factories and workers' settlements that provided a template for future worker communities throughout Britain for decades to come (even a Sunday School was built for the workers' children). Stretching along the river and throughout the surrounding valley for 24 km from Matlock Bath to Derby, these mills are considered to be the birthplace of the modern factory, where water power was first used to power complex mechanised processes, and have been a UNESCO World Heritage Site since 2001, as examples of 'industrial archaeology'. A silk mill was built in Derby at the southern end of the valley in 1721, but it wouldn't be until the 1770s and the growth in importance of cotton that the ground-breaking inventions of Richard

Photo: SteveLewis76

Arkwright transformed this sleepy corner of Derbyshire into the epicentre of Britain's new Industrial Age, aided by his invention of a new water frame for spinning cotton, and a carding engine able to turn raw cotton into cotton lap.

The series of mills that were built to house these machines were impressive in themselves. The Cromford Mill (1771), now a Grade I listed building, was the first to be built, a five-storey building for 200 workers. A second mill followed at Belper, south of Cromford (which burned down in 1890), and then a third – Masson Mill (1783) – was designed with centrally located staircases so the production floor could be freed up to take more of Arkwright's machines. Many of these buildings survived the decline of the cotton industry – including the terraced housing on North Street at Cromford (1776), the Cromford marketplace (1790), and its Greyhound Hotel (1778) – and have been sensitively repurposed. Masson Mill is now a textile museum housing the world's largest collection of bobbins, while the buildings at Belper have been converted to various business uses.

Leaving the mills the trail continues from Belper via Little Eaton and into Derby where it follows the River Derwent and becomes the 'Riverside Path' before leading on to a bridleway to Elvaston Castle, a beautiful Gothic Revival manor house surrounded by 200 acres of woodlands and formal gardens. The path, now on the south bank of the river, passes through Borrowash and the time-capsule town of Shardlow, probably the best surviving example of a British 'canal town' with over 50 Grade II listed buildings. The trail now follows the Trent and Mersey Canal along its towpath to Derwent Mouth, where the River Derwent merges with the River Trent, and where your walk through the valley – which did more than any other to give shape to our modern industrial world – comes to an end.

23. ISLE OF MAN COASTAL PATH
Isle of Man

Distance: 153 km
Grade: Strenuous
Time: 5–7 days

Created to celebrate the Isle of Man's Heritage Year celebrations in 1986, the 153-km-long Isle of Man Coastal Path – the Raad ny Foillan, the 'Way of the Gull' – encircles the entire Manx coast, from the extensive dune systems, glens and shingle beaches of the north and 600-ft-high cliffs in the west, to the rugged cliffs and moorlands of the south, and leads towards Cashtal yn Ard (Castle of the Heights) in the east, the largest Neolithic tomb of its kind in the British Isles. When the trail is forced to take to the island's roads they are as much a blessing as a curse, with little traffic to interfere with the sensory delights around you. You are never far from the ocean, of course, never far from the 'cry of the gull'. And never far, also, from reminders that you are in a different world – the world of the 'Manx' - the result of hundreds of years of Celtic/Norse migration followed by Irish influences which eventually gave birth to the Manx language – Manx Gaelic – which still undergoes its periodic revivals. Envelopes won't get off the island unless a Manx stamp is affixed to it, and the Manx pound is the island's currency. It is a proud, independent heritage you cannot help but be aware of as you walk a coastline that is treated as a prized asset by the island's residents.

Here you can be in no doubt you are walking along the same high coastal ground where the first hunter gatherers of

Photo: Badgernet

the Middle Stone Age would have lived in tiny huts, and who would have looked across at the same crumbling cliffs of Orrisdale Head north of Peel as you do. Neolithic and Bronze Age arrivals brought farming, pottery, and a scattering of megalithic monuments such as King Orry's grave at Laxey. There is no evidence the Romans ever came here, but the Vikings and Druids did, and so did Pictish seafarers, who chose to settle here and then became farmers – when they weren't conducting raids on Roman Britain as the dreaded 'painted men'.

The Isle of Man Coastal Path starts and finishes at the Millennium Bridge in the island's capital of Douglas, population 30,000 – a far cry from the tiny settlement of 1511 when a mere thirteen households were documented north of the harbour. It is easily walked in sections, if that is all you have time to do, and each place name that indicates a sectional starting point is well serviced by the island's network of buses. But to walk the entire circuit takes only a week at most, which makes it a very real consideration if one wants to 'complete' a trail rather than attempting only part of the usual long distance footpaths and National Trail options.

An eclectic mix of views and experiences await you on this varied trail. The path skirts the boundary of Ronaldsway Airport near Derbyhaven and passes over the site of the 1275 battle on which the Manx kingdom lost its independence to the Scots for a hundred years until the English arrived and supplanted them. Between St Johns and Ramsey you'll walk along the trackbed of the abandoned Manx Northern Railway, and there is a long and very pretty section of pebbly beach from Ramsey to Point of Ayre, the path's northernmost point where you'll find the Point of Ayre lighthouse, the island's oldest lighthouse (1818) designed and built by Robert Stevenson, the grandfather of author Robert Louis Stevenson. On the east coast, while in Laxey be sure to detour to the famous Laxey waterwheel, the largest in existence, and also walk to Dhoon Glen, a gorgeous wooded glen just north of Laxey with steep inclines that will make you 'work' for the views!

If you want to make the most of your stay on the island there are three other marked trails worth considering: the half-day Heritage Trail (16 km, easy) inland from Douglas across to Peel following the old Douglas to Peel railway line; a full day's hike along the Herring Trail (22.5 km, easy) from Peel inland via Glen Maye to Castletown in the south once used by the island's fishermen; and the Millennium Way from Ramsey to Castletown running north-south down the island's interior, a path once used by the Manx King, and first documented in the 13th-century *Chronicles of the Kings of Mann*. And that's a lot of history for one very small island.

22. WEST HIGHLAND WAY
East Dunbartonshire to Highland, Scotland

Distance: 153 km
Grade: Easy
Time: 8 days

Scotland's first and still most popular long distance trail begins in Milngavie to the north of Glasgow and finishes at Fort William at the base of Ben Nevis, a total of 153 km. It was first thought of in the 1930s and brought to fruition in 1980, hastened by the success of the Pennine Way. Conceived as a south to north trail, this is the direction most choose to walk, seduced by some beguiling detours along the way due to its proximity to so many of Scotland's most alluring peaks such as Ben Lomond and Ben Nevis. It is a walk of contrasts – contrasts in landscapes, geology, flora and fauna – and everywhere there are traces of human habitation – trails that were once ancient droving roads, or roads built in an effort to contain Jacobite clansmen – roads that have been followed by contemporary ribbons of bitumen or are estate drives or forestry roads, and yet only rarely does the presence of passing automobiles impinge on the sense of being 'in the wild'.

The West Highland Way doesn't just pass through places, it passes through history. The lands of the Earls of Lennox, a fiefdom of sorts in the 1300s that was distinct from the seven Provinces of Scotland; Breadalbane with its Neolithic chambered cairns, its cup-and-ring carved stones and thousands of cup-marked rocks, standing stones and stone circles of the late Neolithic and Middle Bronze Ages; and Lochaber, with its wealth of castle ruins and that engineering marvel of the early 19th century, the 97-km-long Caledonian Canal, linking Scotland's east coast at Inverness with the west coast at Corpach north of Fort William on Loch Linnhe.

The trail is a fabulous introduction to everything Scottish. It skirts the shoreline of Loch Lomond, Great Britain's largest expanse of inland water, the considered boundary between the lowlands of central Scotland and the highlands to the north. It passes under the craggy summit of Ben Lomond (974 m), Scotland's most southerly Munro. It crosses Rannoch Moor, a world of blanket bogs and lochans, of grouse and red deer. A Special Area of Conservation, Rannoch Moor is one of Europe's last unspoiled wildernesses and while walking here brings with it a rare sense of tranquillity and isolation, poor weather can turn it into a quagmire underfoot. But what would any walk in these parts be without muddied boots?

It is also a trail that is best walked in its entirety, if you are able to afford the time to do so, so as to fully appreciate more closely its highlights such as Buachaille Etive Mor, an unassailable-looking summit and one of Scotland's most photographed Munros. There is the gorgeous U-shaped Glen Coe (Scotland's most beautiful glen?) formed by Ice Age glaciers and surrounded on three sides by spectacular, wild, precipitous mountains. The Devil's Staircase, a trail over the Aonach Eagach is climbed and then followed by a descent to Loch Leven, a full circuit of which is possible after years of planning on what is now the Loch Leven Heritage Trail. The Lairig, once the main route south from Fort William but long since bypassed, is now a rather desolate, dramatic passage with Glen Nevis on one side, Loch Leven on the other, and the Mamore Mountains and Ben Nevis – Scotland's highest peak at 1,344 m – filling the horizon before you. Once past Glen Nevis, home to Steall Falls (Scotland's second-highest waterfall with a 120-m drop), you come to the settlement of Fort William, itself a crossroads of several great trails, and the end of your traverse.

And its practicalities? Walking south to north means you'll have the sun at your back, and the wind and rain either behind you or to your left instead of hitting you in your face. As to when to go, while July and August are the warmest months they are not necessarily the driest which is why it's worth considering the 'compromise' period of May/June when you're less likely to get wet, and it is a time when visibility can be exceptional, and the temperatures can be pleasantly warm-ish, even if higher elevations might have lingering snow lines. In May/June there is also less

Photo: Martin Thoma

demand on accommodation, which is surprisingly plentiful considering how isolated walking the trail can feel. There are various B&Bs, three hostels (Rowardennan, Crianlarich and Glen Nevis), bunkhouses, private hostels, campgrounds, even wigwams – simple wooden shelters capable of sleeping up to six people and found mostly on private farms.

Naturally once in Fort William the choices of where to lay one's head take a turn for the better – the Victorian charm of Ashburn House and the five-star comforts of Crolinnhe B&B with its extensive gardens come to mind. Or maybe not? Maybe, now that you're sitting beside the bronze sculpture of a weary walker at the end of the High Street that marks the trail's official start/end point, your appetite sufficiently whetted for highland walking, your thoughts might turn to the trail that *starts* here – the 117-km trail to Inverness, the Great Glen Way?

21. MORAY COAST TRAIL
Moray, Scotland

Distance: 70 km
Grade: Easy
Time: 3 days

Blessed with a variety of topography and wildlife that would be the envy of many a British coastal trail, from seals, otters and osprey to wildfowl and the always present Moray Firth dolphins, the Moray Coast Trail can begin or end at the town of Findhorn, or further afield though slightly inland at Forres, utilising a well-maintained bicycle trail. Forres is one of Scotland's oldest towns, and from there all the way to the charming fishing village of Cullen, with its expansive sandy beach and ruins of Findlater Castle, you'll have views over the vastness of the Moray Firth and the North Sea with its collection of skerries and coves visible from an exposed coastline that offers little sanctuary should the weather turn nasty. So don't forget to pack the waterproofs.

This three-day trail is a delightful mix of beaches, coastal paths, virtually car-free roads, and old rail lines and ridges, and while you are never too far from civilisation in a region with a rich tapestry of human settlement, this mostly level trail with only a few steepish climbs still manages to possess an overwhelming sense of quiet – even of wilderness.

Entirely covered by public right of access and presuming you travel west to east, you can begin at Forres – the accepted site of Duncan's castle from Shakespeare's *Macbeth* – and head for the coast at Findhorn (or take a bus for this section if pressed for time). Look out for red squirrels as you pass through Roseisle Forest on your way to Burghead, the first of numerous old fishing villages to come.

Leaving Burghead you pass the Diageo maltings plant before joining an old rail line that follows the coast to the town of Cummingston and on to Hopeman and its array of colourful beach huts. A grassy section of rising coastline then descends to the lovely and oft-deserted Clashach Cove, with its interesting backdrop of cliffs which are all that remains of an ancient fossilised dune system incorporating some nicely exposed fossilised footprints of early reptiles if you pause long enough to look for them. It's then up and along a ridge above Covesea Quarry (look for nesting fulmars in its sandstone cliffs) and a glimpse of Covesea Lighthouse ahead before another ascent takes you up and around a sandy bay

Photo: Lawsonstu

from which you descend on to a stretched-out arc of a beach and a cup of tea at Covesea's Tee Shack Cafe.

Working your way towards Covesea lighthouse you soon have a gorgeous, uninterrupted walk along 2 km of sandy beach before reaching the village of Lossiemouth, with its charming harbour at the mouth of the River Lossie. You then cross the Spynie Canal to Seatown, better known in days gone by as Dogwall because of the dogfish skins that were hung out to dry around its harbour. The dune system here is particularly interesting, a man-made collection of sandy hills that have been encouraged to accumulate thanks to the clever placement of old railway carriages, and which protect the town from fierce North Sea storms. If you're walking here in late spring or early summer you're likely to pass nesting terns as well as the remnants of gun emplacements and even tank traps, now mostly hidden in gorse bushes, built in the 1940s to deter a German invasion that never came.

After just over two hours' walking on from Lossiemouth you'll enter a military firing range where a red flag, if it is flying, means the range is active and you'll have to leave the coastal path and take an alternative route via Binn Hill before joining up with the path again on the far side of the range. (Firing dates can be confirmed ahead of time by contacting the Binn Hill Range Warden.) Assuming you negotiate the range without incident you'll then pass through a barren area near the town of Kingston made all but lifeless over a thirty year period beginning in the mid-1930s when shingle was mined to make concrete. The mine closed in the 1970s, however, and since then life has returned with skylarks, plovers, and assorted species of butterfly as well as native plants and grasses gaining an increasingly impressive foothold. Walk on through Kingston and continue to Garmouth, near the mouth of the River Spey and a town with an impressive royal connection. It was here on 23 June 1650 that King James II signed the Solemn League and Covenant, the agreement between Scottish Covenanters and English Parliamentarians guaranteeing Scottish support in the fight against Irish Catholic 'papists'.

Crossing the Spey over an old railway bridge that once groaned under the weight of locomotives, such as the Great North of Scotland Railway's No 49 *Gordon Highlander*, you merge with the Speyside Way, one of Scotland's four official Long Distance Routes. The trail takes you to Spey Bay where you might be fortunate enough to spot its colony of bottlenose dolphins before continuing on the waymarked trail through a pine forest and on to a farm track, returning to the old rail line and joining a sealed road that will take you back to the coast and into Portgordon, established as a fishing village by Alexander Gordon, the 4th Duke of Gordon, in 1797.

At Portgordon the trail returns to the coast where it's only 2 km to the fishing village of Buckie and a brief stint on the A942 before circling Cluny Harbour and returning to the A942 to Portessie and Strathlene Sands. A nice walk along a rocky foreshore is followed by a small ascent to a ridgeline (keep the Strathlene golf course to your right) before descending once more to the coast and the inlet near Findochty, with its nicely protected harbour and disused lighthouse. If you decide to linger here you won't be disappointed: its surrounding cliffs are home to a myriad of seabirds, the area is honeycombed with various caves and inlets, and the remains of Findochty Castle are worth exploring.

A cycle path takes you from Sandy Creek on the eastern side of Findochty up to the ridges around Tronach Head and on to Cliff Terrace on the outskirts of clifftop-dwelling Portknockie, founded in 1677 with the old town's collection of north-south aligning single-storey stone houses forming the centrepiece of the 'Portknockie Experience' – a guided historic walk. Now essentially a residential community, the present harbour dates to 1890 and the town has managed to retain a modest fishing fleet. Leaving Portknockie you look down on Bow Fiddle Rock, an offshore wave-cut natural arch that looks like the hull of an upturned navy destroyer and is a roosting place for seagulls and cormorants, before descending to the beach with views to the Whale's Moo, an impressive sea cave, and Preacher's Cave, used as a secret meeting place by the Free Church after its break with the Church of Scotland in the 1840s.

From here you round the promontory and the broad sweep of Cullen Bay comes into view. Make for the clubhouse of the local golf course and climb the stairs into the huddled enclave of Cullen Seatown and from there into the township of Cullen itself, walking under the famous Cullen Viaducts on the way. While in Cullen make sure you take the 9-km return walk to the 14th-century ruins of Findlater Castle, perched on a quartz-encrusted promontory to the east of town. The ruins can be accessed via a narrow path leading down from the headland but care is needed on the descent, and the ruins themselves are in a somewhat parlous state.

And whether you're starting or finishing in Cullen, don't leave town without trying their local Cullen Skink, that most wonderful of northeastern Scottish everyday dishes comprising smoked haddock, onions and mashed potatoes in a thick milky, fishy soup not unlike a good north eastern United States clam chowder. Usually served as a starter, it also sits nicely in a thermos, and so makes a heart-warming walking companion on those cool, Moray Firth days.

20. SYDNEY HARBOUR BRIDGE CLIMB
Sydney, Australia

Distance: Negligible
Grade: Easy
Time: 2 hours

If you should ever find yourself in Sydney, Australia, and you either need or would like to cross Sydney Harbour from north to south, or vice-versa, several choices confront you. You can take a water taxi, catch a ferry, or even hop on a train. If you have a car you can either drive *under* the harbour via the harbour tunnel – a claustrophobic experience at best – or you can do what I always choose to do: you can drive across the Sydney Harbour Bridge. After all why suffer a tunnel when you can immerse yourself in a sculpture?

Like hundreds of thousands of fellow Sydney-siders and throngs of gaping tourists every year, I never tire of looking at this bridge Australians affectionately call 'the Coathanger' and never cease to be impressed by its scale, by its sheer audacity. Completed in 1932 it took 1,400 men eight years to build, a significantly 'over-engineered' triumph that was at the time as advanced as any bridge anywhere in the world. Before it opened, the government shunted 96 steam locomotives on to it for one final check of its load-bearing capacity, and in its first year 11,000 cars a day crossed between its granite pylons. Now that figure is closing in on 200,000 cars a day. At times the bridge with its graceful arch-to-arch span of 503 m – after 84 years still the sixth-longest-spanning arch bridge in the world – seems to groan under its eight lanes of traffic and two rail lines and all the weight

of expectations we place upon it. It can be a noisy old bridge, and like bustling urban environments everywhere, it's always good to get above it. If you can.

In 1998, after years of struggling with government red tape and overcoming every conceivable objection, Bridge Climb was born. At last, one would be able to do more than just cross the bridge along its pedestrian pathways, suffering a stiff neck from all that looking 'up'. Now Bridge Climb – the city's only licensed bridge climb operator – can take you on a meandering journey up through this intricate steel skeleton, walking over perforated steel grilles and climbing up four near-vertical steel ladders that look as though they'd be more at home on a navy destroyer than on a piece of urban architecture, while being tethered every step of the way by means of a stainless steel cable that runs from the harness strapped over the blue Bridge Suit that you've crawled into in the preparation area to a cable runner attached to the bridge itself.

Bridge Climb is typical of how existing pieces of urban infrastructure the world over – from bridges to canal towpaths to disused rail lines – are being re-imagined and adapted to provide us with ever-increasing access to our built environments. After suiting up in the cavernous preparation area you leave accessories like mobile phones and (reluctantly for this camera-addicted traveller) my Canon 6D in your locker, complete a safety check and from there you walk through a purpose-built tunnel before emerging into the bridge's superstructure and starting your approach to the summit along the bridge's upper arch.

Making your way towards your goal – the arch's 134-m summit above the calm waters of the world's most beautiful harbour – you'd be forgiven for thinking the whole thing is more a climb than a walk. But the exercise is an exhilarating one. On the final approach to the centre of the bridge's great steel arc the harbour city opens up before you in all of its 360-degree splendour, and you see it for the very first time from a perspective you never thought you would. If you live here it's like being introduced for the first time to a distant relative you always knew you'd had, but had never met. Yet the sense of familiarity once on it is overwhelming. The Sydney Opera House and Circular Quay are below you to your right, with the CBD (Central Business District) and the Botanic Gardens behind them. Looking east you can see all the way to Watson's Bay and beyond towards South Head, west past Goat Island to where the harbour begins to narrow to form the Parramatta River, and north over the sprawling cluster of apartment blocks that cover the hills of North Sydney that was once a gorgeous sea of Federation and Victorian residences, long since gone.

It is not something everyone can do. If you're 24 weeks pregnant or more you'll need a certificate of fitness from your doctor, and if you're under ten years of age or not quite 1.2 m high then unfortunately you'll have to bide your time. And you can't take cameras or cell phones, either. But if you're going to be concerned about anything, why not consider the 1,332 steps you'll have to negotiate, and before long you'll be grateful you left all your accessories – with the exception of sunglasses – behind.

What the walk lacks in distance (from the preparation area to the summit wouldn't be more than 400 m when all the early twists and turns are ironed out) it makes up for in a vertigo-inducing final approach to the top. After a group photograph and a few minutes where you're left to yourself to contemplate life, the universe and everything, you then cross to the other side of the bridge across its 'spine' where you can pause to look down to the eight lanes of traffic that is the Bradfield Highway before descending along the bridge's western arch back towards its twin southern pylons, and the end of one memorable urban walk.

19. COAST TO COAST WALK
Cumbria, North Yorkshire, England

Distance: 309 km
Grade: Moderate
Time: 14 days

Alfred Wainwright was born in Blackburn, Lancashire, in 1907. He excelled at school, studied accountancy, enjoyed cartography to the point of drawing his own set of local maps, and got a job at Blackburn Borough Council. At the age of 23 he had saved enough money to embark on a week's walking through the Lake District with his cousin Eric Beardsall. Upon climbing Orrest Head (238 m) on the eastern shoreline of Windermere the young Alfred saw the Lakeland Fells for the first time, and what he saw transfixed him – an expanse of mountains, woodlands and lakes stretching, it seemed, to infinity, a serene world he later described as being 'in a tumultuous array across glittering waters; our awakening to beauty'. Over the next decades Wainwright did more than anyone to promote the tradition of fell walking. His pictorial guide to the Lakeland Fells, a series of seven guidebooks published from 1952 to 1966, remains the Lake District's standard reference on fells and the trails that connect them. He later went on to write a guidebook on the Pennine Way, and in 1973 devised and wrote a new book about a long distance walk across northern England he had cobbled together on his own starting at St Bees, south of St Bees Head in Cumbria on the Irish Sea and ending at Robin Hood's Bay, 9 km south of Whitby on the North Sea. He titled his new book, appropriately, *A Coast to Coast Walk*.

Described as a masterpiece, and even smacking of genius, the walk bisects three very different national parks – the Lake District National Park, the Yorkshire Dales National Park and the North York Moors National Park – and was originally envisaged as a series of stages with an extra day here and there for sightseeing or just plain 'staring' (Wainwright was fond of the idea of 'standing and staring', a pastime capable of adding considerable time to any walk – and playing havoc with itineraries!). He was also averse to people following precisely the route he had created for himself, preferring them instead to follow his suggestions but find their own way just as he had done, to deviate from prescribed pathways and make their own individual, unique memories.

Walking the Coast to Coast from west to east, Wainwright recommended dipping your boots in the Irish Sea at St Bees and again in the North Sea at Robin Hood's Bay, just so you could *truly* say you went 'coast to coast', and the west-to-east option remains the more popular route as it places the prevailing winds at your back, and the late afternoon sun over your shoulder, perfect for photographs. Some, however, may prefer to walk east to west and make the Lake District the culmination of their crossing.

Those who are content, however, to walk in Wainwright's footsteps will not be disappointed. The Coast to Coast Walk takes a high level route wherever possible, whether it be

Photo: Kreuzschnabel

over the Westmorland limestone plateau, over the Pennines watershed, the Gunnerside and Melbeck moors or over the heather-clad highlands of the North York Moors. If you looked to walk the perfect line between its chosen start and end points, you could do no better than take the almost ruler-straight route Wainwright devised.

From St Bees Head you set off north along its sandstone cliffs before turning east through the West Cumberland Plains towards the western boundaries of the Lake District National Park, and a demanding climb up Dent Fell (352 m), then descending on a forestry track down to the valley of Nanny Catch Beck and ending a tough day (with an accumulated elevation gain of around 1,100 m!) at Ennerdale Bridge. A path around Ennerdale Water leads to a dirt track and after 6.5 km you enter Ennerdale Valley. An old tramway path takes you into Honister, through lovely Johnny's Wood, and into Rosthwaite. The Cumbria Way takes you through the Borrowdale Valley and past impressive Eagle Crag before climbing to Greenup Edge and trailing along Helm Crag Ridge to Grasmere, one-time home to William Wordsworth.

Climbing to Grisedale Hause a choice of three trails of varying difficulty now presents itself, all ending in the town of Patterdale. Next comes Kidsty Pike – the walk's high point at 780 m with its wonderfully angled profile and long considered a fell in its own right despite its connection to its parent peak, Rampsgill Head. Descending to Haweswater and rounding its lake you leave the Lake District and find yourself on the limestone pavements of the Westmorland limestone plateau that take you into the small market town of Kirkby Stephen on the banks of the River Eden.

Climbing again, this time up to England's primary watershed at Nine Standards Rigg where moorland paths descend to the lovely town of Swaledale, you are now at the half-way point where the trail crosses the Pennine Way at the village of Keld, from which a high route and low route both lead to Reeth and on to the market town of Richmond. It's then across the flat pasturelands of the Vale of Mowbray and along the western boundary of the North York Moors, one of the UK's largest expanses of heather moorland – a gorgeous mix of plateaus, dales, woodlands and farms. The trail joins here with the Cleveland Way and the interesting and little-known Lyke Wake Walk, first suggested as a trail by a local farmer in 1955 who argued it was possible to walk on nothing but heather over a 40-mile (64-km) route across the moors of northeast Yorkshire at their highest point.

Next is Urra Moor, the North York Moors' highest at 454 m, and turning north from here at Bloworth Crossing places you on the tracks of the Rosedale Railway, opened in 1861 to transport iron ore deposits then being mined in the Rosedale Valley. The rail line closed in 1929, but a section that runs up to Blakey Junction is followed before continuing to Glaisdale, home to the lovely Beggar's Bridge (1619) and a mere 13 km west of Whitby. With the end in sight, a woodland path takes you into Egton Bridge, host to England's oldest gooseberry festival, and a disused tollroad leads into the village of Grosmont and through Littlebeck on the River Esk. On the clifftops of the north coast it links up again with the Cleveland Way before paralleling the coast south to your final destination, Robin Hood's Bay.

18. HADRIAN'S WALL PATH
Tyne and Wear to Cumbria, England

Distance: 135 km
Grade: Easy
Time: 7 days

When Julius Caesar travelled to Britain in 55 and 54 BCE he wasn't interested in conquest, instead simply initiating a period of looting and collecting of tributes, and perhaps gaining along the way a little prestige in the eyes of his conquered Gallic opponents. Caesar's successor, the Emperor Augustus, showed little interest in occupying Britain after his advisors convinced him (mistakenly, it would turn out) it would require sending an entire legion there, and that its maintenance would be greater than could be collected in tributes and taxes. Claudius sent four legions to Britain in 43 CE, mined its lead and shipped its cereals over the channel to his army on the Rhine. By the time Publius Aelius Hadrianus was born in 76 CE, southern Britain was divided into local jurisdictions and was firmly under Rome's control. Its far flung provinces in Wales and northern Britain were securely garrisoned, and a network of roads criss-crossed the British countryside, with watchtowers and forts at their junctions.

When Hadrian became Emperor in 117 CE incursions by Caledonian Picts into northern Britain were resulting in a continuing flow of casualties, and the north's mountainous terrain was not providing comfort to the Roman cause. So in 122 CE Hadrian crossed the channel and went north to the River Tyne where he ordered construction of the Pons

Aelius – a bridge and fort complex on the river. Itself a marvel of Roman engineering it would be the only bridge outside of Rome to carry the imperial epithet – a hint to its strategic importance. But Hadrian hadn't come to Tyne just to inaugurate the building of a bridge. He envisaged a limestone wall, 4 m high and 3 m thick, made from locally quarried stone with rubble and mortar at its centre that would stretch across Britain from the banks of the River Tyne in the east to the Solway Firth on the Irish Sea (the section west from the River Irthing would originally have comprised turf, with stone added later). There would be milecastles (small forts garrisoning up to 60 men) at every Roman mile (a thousand paces made up of two steps, as marched by Roman armies), a series of sixteen forts with large gates facing north at points in the wall where roads passed through, plus turrets and crenellated parapets. Hadrian had given up on the idea of eastward expansion so beloved of his predecessor Trajan, dismantling the Roman bridge over the Danube and surrendering Roman gains in Mesopotamia, and had turned his gaze closer to home. Some eight years later his wall across Britain would be complete, a monument to the far flung limits of empire.

The wall – supplemented by a ditch on its north side, and the 'vallum', an earthwork on its southern side – was built not merely to deter invaders, but to help regulate the flow of people already under Roman rule and so maintain control of existing territories *south* of the wall. In a way, it was more a 'fence' than a defensive wall, and while the strategic priorities behind its construction might be the subject of some scholarly debate, what is certain is that while much of the wall is long gone, sections of Hadrian's Wall have survived in somewhat spectacular style, no mean feat considering it stood idle for more than seven centuries after the Romans finally abandoned it. Over several centuries and as late as the early 20th century people were pillaging its stones to use in other buildings. The fact there's still a wall to follow is due in no small part to Newcastle-upon-Tyne's 19th-century town clerk and antiquarian John Clayton (1782–1890) who, in 1834, began buying up sections of the wall from Chesters all the way to the border with Cumbria (then Cumberland) to keep its stones from being removed. His enthusiasm was a major reason for the sections in and around Chesters, Housesteads and Vindolanda being in such excellent states of preservation today.

Ever since the trail's 'resurgence' in the 19th century thoughts had been entertained that a path might be built to follow it. The 8th-century earthwork that gave rise to Offa's Dyke Path in 1971, however, failed to give the impetus to its construction that some had hoped. In fact it wouldn't be until 2003 that Britain's fifteenth Long Distance Path was at last inaugurated, stretching for 135 km across northern England and for the most part closely following the ancient wall, the finest surviving example of frontier work in all of Rome's classical period. There are just two segments where the path substantially deviates: roughly from milecastles 0–12 where it follows a river, and again through Carlisle following another riverbank. It can be a muddy slog at times, but the trail is well signposted and the walking straightforward and undemanding. There are six stages, beginning in the east with Wallsend to Heddon-on-the-Wall (24 km), then on to Chollerford (25 km), Steel Rigg (19 km), Walton (25 km), Carlisle (18 km), and Bowness-on-Solway (24 km).

But which way to walk? Scholars determined long ago that the wall was built 'east to west', but the savvy walker will be aware that the best direction to cross is from west to east, so that the prevailing winds will hit your back and not your face

Photo: Johnnie Shannon

(also, the sun being behind you for the greater part of the day makes for much better photographs).

The wall itself can be divided into four states of preservation: Consolidated, where English Heritage have worked to consolidate it using mortar; Clayton, those sections repaired under the direction of John Clayton using the dry stone method with turf on top; Semi-field, genuine wall remnants in the form of small foundational sections or individual stones; and Rubble Rigg, linear mounds in situ where the masonry has been stolen. Archaeological sites are, of course, everywhere, and are reason enough to add a few days to any proposed itinerary. There is Segedunum, the wall's most excavated fort that stood for 300 years and once housed 600 soldiers; Corbridge, a Roman town and supply base where you can walk on the very same road – the Stanegate – where Roman feet once trod; and Vindolanda Fort, which predated the wall and served as an important construction site, distributing supplies to the new wall. The site of the wall's only ongoing archaeological dig, the wooden 'writing tablets' found at Vindolanda and dating to between 85 CE and 160 CE, which were unearthed by archaeologists while excavating a drainage ditch in 1972, are especially worth a look, giving as they do a rare glimpse into the sort of everyday conversations the Roman garrisons and their families had.

The Senhouse Roman Museum overlooking the Solway Firth, with its precious collection of military altars, funerary monuments, Celtic sculptures and Roman pottery is also a must-visit, as is Chesters Roman Fort in Northumberland, Britain's most complete Roman cavalry fort with exceptionally well-preserved baths, steam room and officer's quarters. There are also a number of English Heritage properties close to the trail, including Prudhoe Castle, Aydon Castle,

Housesteads, Carlisle Castle, and the best-preserved of all Cumbrian monasteries – Lanercost Priory.

Be mindful, too, that when you come here you are walking over a fragile landscape. The greatest enemy of the wall has always been erosion, and foot traffic is increasing along the trail every year. Over 90 per cent of the original curtainwall has already been lost over time, not an ideal statistic, but the fact it hasn't been horribly tampered with in a clumsy attempt to reconstruct it is a blessing. What makes walking the path so memorable is the sense that you are walking alongside a relic that is authentic and *real*. Pilfered, worn down, showing its age – yes it is all of this. But it is genuine.

Make sure that if you're in a group you avoid walking in single file – spread your footsteps broadly so no one line of the path becomes excessively worn. Well-grassed paths provide cover and drainage for fragile earthworks below. And please, though it is tempting, resist the urge to walk on the wall itself. Although chamfered stones – those tell-tale shapes associated with crenellated walls – have been uncovered here, and there are steps present at Milecastle 48, suggesting soldiers may have in fact walked on top of the wall, there are no excuses for continuing the practice! And there are two full-height reconstructions of the wall – at Vindolanda and Wallsend – if one is keen to experience what walking on it was like.

The highest portions of the wall can be found 500 m east of Milecastle 42 at Thorny Doors, and at Hare Hill in Cumbria where a section became a part of a medieval structure before being rebuilt in the 19th century. Where the wall is gone altogether, the trail is well signposted to keep you on track. Fortunately, too, Ancient Rome is not the only point of interest here: the north bank of the Tyne, the wild escarpments of Whin Sill, the pastures of Cumbria, the salt marshes of the

Solway Estuary, the path's brief linking up with the Pennine Way – all this means there is also plenty of Great Britain herself – *Provincia Britannia* – to vie for your attention.

17. PAPA STOUR
Shetland Islands, Scotland

Distance: Variable
Grade: Easy
Time: 1 day

If you like following your nose along heavily eroded coastlines – coastlines that have been battered and bludgeoned by waves, storms and winds for millennia and carved into fantastical sea stacks, arches, skerries and enthralling natural features like Kirstan Hol, the world's fourth-longest sea cave, and where bare bands of pink rhyolite and solidified lava have been laid bare along its coastal rock faces – then you need to come here, to Papa Stour, at the southwestern end of St Magnus Bay to the west of mainland Shetland.

It is the *Papey Stora* of the Vikings, the 'large island of priests' in Old Norse – a nod to the small community of Celtic missionaries who once called it home. A handy stopover for Norsemen who found safe anchorage here, the island had become a Norwegian royal farm by the end of the 13th century and these new incumbents, once established, proved difficult to dislodge. Norwegian estates remained on Papa Stour until well into the 17th century, despite the Shetlands being ceded to Scotland in 1469! Papa Stour also produced the Shetlands' oldest written extant document, a

1299 petition detailing local grievances. And let's not forget the abundant evidence of human habitation dating back to Neolithic and Bronze Age communities. History aplenty, if you know where to look for it.

A wall known as the Hill Dyke separates the gravelly sub-soil of the heathlands of the north and west with its covering of thyme, spring squill, woolly hair mosses and heath-spotted orchids from the more fertile land in the east. The island is remarkably flat, with Virda Field at just 87 m its high point, providing a glorious panorama. On the hill behind the island's primary school you'll find a series of Neolithic burial chambers, while the remains of several vertical shaft water mills can be found around Dutch Loch. At Da Biggins an archaeological dig has unearthed the foundations of a 13th-century Norse house – a *stofa* – a timber building constructed with notched logs that was smaller than most Viking longhouses though larger than the homes of the average Shetlander. In 2008 the Papa Stour History Group built a reconstruction of a *stofa* at the site, using logs imported from Norway. At Housa Voe a circle of 36 stones suggests the presence of a local assembly, and in later centuries lepers were banished here from the mainland and forced to live in isolation in the south of the island, kept alive by the generosity of Papa Stour's residents. Now that's a lot of history for one tiny little island.

If you like walking solo and tire of having to nod your head to a flotilla of passers-by then Papa Stour is what you've been looking for thanks to a resident population of something around 20, the majority of whom make a living from traditional crofting. The population reached a peak of almost 400 in the 19th century when a fishing port was established at West Voe on the southern tip of Shetland, but soon began to steadily decline.

Photo: Doug Lee

Photo: low cloud

To get here you can catch the inter-island ferry from West Burrafirth, which operates five days a week and takes around 40 minutes in good weather, to Housa Voe ('House Bay'). There is a car ferry also – the *Snolda* – but as there's only one road on the island, and a short one at that, best just leave the car behind – and lace up your walking boots. If you want to stay overnight then you'd better bring a tent as there is no accommodation.

The island has 35 km of rugged, heavily indented coastline but it is its west coast, exposed to the wilds of the Atlantic, that is its most crenellated. There are no marked walking trails on its 828 hectares, but they are hardly needed – the coastline is all you need and you can't lose your bearings. A short walk from the ferry terminal and you're passing headlands and blowholes and charming little bays that just keep on beckoning. The erosive power of water is seen in J-shaped indents such as Jerome Coutts' Head, while other incursions into the landscape, like the Creed, lead to tranquil bodies of calm water. A path of sorts leads you around the island's southern shore past the Hill of Feilie, where you'll get a grand view of Sandness Hill across the Sound of Papa, and don't miss the bizarre leaning offshore rock that is Clingri Geo, a drunken-looking partially collapsed rock with a tunnel through it to the sea. One of the island's most prominent landmarks, a sea stack called the Horn of Papa, was swept away in a storm in 1953. Plenty of lovely stacks remain, though, including Snolda Stack and Aesha Stack with its gorgeous natural arch.

Geos – linear sea cliff clefts that showcase marine erosion along lines of weakness – are common here where fractured rocks are so susceptible to wave erosion – and always worth walking to just to watch the interplay between the rock and the Atlantic's angry, churning waters. One of Papa Stour's most intriguing geos is Christie's Hole, a labyrinth of tunnels and collapsed caverns so extensive that in 1981 a depression on the surface above one of its caverns collapsed. Rockfalls are common in Papa Stour's geos, evidence that they are still growing and fracturing.

The island also provides an ideal environment for ground-nesting birds such as Arctic terns and skuas, while more than a dozen species of sea birds including kittiwakes, guillemots, fulmars and razorbills nest in its abundant sea cliffs on some of the most impressive stretches of coastline the Shetlands have to offer, on an island that intrigues on so many levels.

16. VIA FRANCIGENA
England / France / Switzerland / Italy

Distance: 1,899 km
Grade: Strenuous
Time: 3 months

One of the great and ancient pilgrimages of Europe, the Via Francigena – 'the road that comes from France' – grew as a devout pathway to Rome in the years after Emperor Constantine issued the Edict of Milan in 313 CE, an agreement to provide Christians with legal status and treat them with 'benevolence'. It started as a collection of local paths and trails of varying quality and widths, maintained by local nobles and linking villages, mountain passes and seaports. Walking it was not without its dangers from bandits, wild animals and disease, and if you walked it as a pilgrim there was a lot to do before you even started: prepare a will, settle all debts, ask forgiveness from all one may have slighted, be dressed in a pilgrim's habit by your local priest or bishop, and lastly, say goodbye to your loved ones. After all, the chances of making it back alive were not exactly encouraging, and even if you did make it back, if you were late in returning by more than a year and a day you were presumed dead, and your property became the property of your heirs.

It entered the historical record for the first time in 725 CE as 'the Frankish route' in the pages of the *Itinerarium sancti Willibaldi*, a travel journal written by the Bavarian Bishop of Eichstatt and inveterate traveller, Saint Willibald. Rather than a central paved road, the trail began as a series of parallel and divergent pathways that altered over time as trading routes came and went. There were several points over which one could cross the Alps and the Apennines, and the 'dots' that joined the route were abbeys and not cities – dots that were more prone to being altered as the centuries progressed. By the close of the first millennium the route consisted of some 80 stages, each around 20 km in length, not dissimilar from the prospect for anyone contemplating walking it today. By the time Sigeric the Serious, then Archbishop of Canterbury, walked from Canterbury to Rome and back again in 990 to receive his Papal pallium – a simple woollen cloak embroidered with six black crosses, the symbol of his investiture – the route had become known as the Via Francigena. Pilgrim numbers increased greatly after 1300, when Pope Boniface VIII announced the first Christian Jubilee, where he would grant afresh 'great remissions and indulgences for sins' for all who came to see him.

The Via Francigena is not nearly as popular as that other historic, much-trampled pilgrimage trail, Spain's Way of St James, a fact due in part to there being fewer places to stay, on average, on this route; therefore any anxiety about whether you will get to a hotel at the end of each day is minimised if you are prepared to pitch a tent. Those who walk its entire length in any given year can vary between 2,000 and 3,000, as opposed to the tens of thousands that walk the Way of St James, which means you'll barely see anyone else doing what you are doing until you reach oft-trod Tuscany. But any who attempt to walk its entire length, or for any who set out to conquer even just a few of its stages, to walk on what was Europe's most significant medieval road will remain a life-changing experience.

Just decades ago the only people interested in the route were scholars. The rebirth of the 'modern' Via Francigena officially occurred in 1985 when the Italian Archaeologist of Roads, Giovanni Caselli, retraced, surveyed and mapped Sigeric's route, as best he could along a road that had lain largely forgotten for centuries. On the way he found tantalising traces of its presence: statues with inscriptions that read: 'I show you the way to Rome', and old Templar churches and monasteries that were able to fill in many of the route's blanks. Pensions and hotels opened their doors to him. Slowly the old road began to take shape, and as awareness of its hoped-for restoration began to circulate, local governments became involved in uncovering and clearing their own sections, and volunteers began dipping brushes into paint tins and marking its trails.

Declared a European Council Cultural Route in 1994, in 2007 a group of cyclists set out from Canterbury Cathedral and rode to Rome in sixteen days, following, more or less, the route redrawn by Caselli. Two years later the Italian government started an initiative to uncover and restore their sections. Other governments soon followed. Walking the Via Francigena today requires a detailed map, as some of its sections are not as clearly marked as they could be. While in

Italy if you're able to obtain a Pilgrim Letter or identity card this will allow you to spend a night in a monastery, convent, or other church building.

You begin in front of Canterbury Cathedral, and from there progress on to the flat expanses that are home to the North Downs Way, and on to Dover. Taking the ferry and alighting in Calais (neglect, if you like, the fact the actual landing point in the Middle Ages was down the coast at Wissant) you head for the Somme and from there to Reims through the vineyards of Champagne and the picturesque hilltop town of Langres. Quiet roads take you into Pontarlier, France's second-highest town, and from there you cross the Swiss border and enter Lausanne on the shores of Lake Geneva. Passing through the famous vineyards at Lavaux with their lineage dating back to the Romans you cross the plains of the Rhone and soon begin your ascent to the town of Martigny (elevation 471 m) at the foot of the Swiss Alps on the eastern boundary of the Rhone Valley. The route into Italy takes you over the Great St Bernard Pass (elevation 2,649 m), Switzerland's third-highest mountain pass and a common route through the Alps since the Bronze Age.

The trail descends into Italy to the city of Aosta, where prayers can be offered in its 4th-century cathedral before heading to Pavia with its wonderful Duomo, and San Pietro in Ciel d'Oro which houses the remains of St Augustine of Hippo, the church's great 5th-century philosopher and theologian. Vercelli on the River Po Plain is home to several Roman relics including a hippodrome and amphitheatre, as well as the Basilica di Sant'Andrea, one of Italy's finest Romanesque structures. You can choose to cross the Po here, just as Sigeric did, by ferry, and continue on to the Ticino Valley Natural Park, a tranquil diversion into Italy's very first regional park established in 1974, a 91,000-acre sanctuary of conifer forests, wetlands, moorlands and farms that is home to 48 mammalian species including badgers, weasels and stone martens.

After crossing the River Po on your way to Piacenza you enter the countryside of Emilia-Romagna, home to Italy's oldest human settlements. The route remains relatively flat and undemanding until you begin the climb into the Apennines where a twisting ascent takes you up to Berceto in the Taro River Valley on the road from La Spezia to Parma.

The route is mostly on woodland trails here as you enter Tuscany after ascending 1,040 m over Cisa Pass near the source of the Magra River, before turning towards the Mediterranean Coast at Sarzana. Then head south through Lucca, San Gimignano and Sienna, staying at refuges in the very same villages Sigeric passed through. South of Sienna the trail parallels another old Roman road, the Via Cassia. The Val d'Orcia Natural Artistic and Cultural Park, created to protect this beautiful valley's cultural and natural heritage while at the same time avoiding turning the region into an open-air museum, is one of the route's most beautiful segments. The final stage from Montefiascone goes via the thermal pools at Bagnaccio and on to the treasure of Viterbo, left largely untouched during World War II with an historic centre that still lies, enchantedly, within its 11th- and 12th-century defensive walls. From here it is a mere 80 km to Rome, via the town of Bagnaia and its relic of aristocratic grandeur, the 16th-century Villa Lante which is also the site of one of Italy's great gardens. Entering Rome you pass the remains of the Etruscan necropolis at Sutri, before weaving your way through a labyrinth of Rome streets, to finish at St Peter's Square in The Vatican.

If you're the sort of person who likes the idea of making a life-changing journey, but are not particularly religious and not so enthusiastic about meeting lines of pilgrims and being coerced into a lot of impromptu chats along the way, then the Via Francigena delivers a perfect balance of socialising and solitude, on a road that, by virtue of walking it, became an act of penitence that delivered those who finished it into the hands of God.

15. TOUR DU MONT BLANC
France / Italy / Switzerland

Distance: 170 km
Grade: Strenuous
Time: 10–12 days

Ever since Horace Benedict de Saussure, the Swiss aristocrat and physicist, set out from Chamonix in 1767 and made his way over the Col du Bonhomme, the Col de la Seigne, Courmayeur, the Great St Bernard Pass, and trekked over the mountains and valleys of the Mont Blanc massif, people have been following in his footsteps. Saussure loved these mountains. In 1760 he offered a reward to the first man to climb Mont Blanc's summit, made his own unsuccessful attempt in 1785, and was the third to conquer it in 1787. He wrote extensively on the massif's topography, its rock strata, even its fossils. He carried thermometers and barometers to the summits of Mont Blanc's surrounding mountains, and his work led him to believe the earth was much older than most had previously thought. Saussure is nowadays considered by many to be not only the founder of modern alpinism, but the man who first brought the Mont Blanc massif's wonders – both scientific and natural – to us all.

People who have never walked a mountain trail have heard of this one and know of its reputation as the finest alpine walk in Europe. The Tour du Mont Blanc (or TMB) will take you around the highest mountain in Europe west of the Caucasus on a 170-km journey through the mountains and valleys of the Mont Blanc massif, with Mont Blanc – *la Dame Blanche*, the 'White Lady' – at the heart of this conglomerate of more than 400 individual mountain peaks as well as glaciers, aiguilles and rock faces any of which would be famous in their own right if they were anywhere else but here. Larger, really, even than a massif, it is a mountain range all on its own. Completing the trail will involve an energy-sapping 10 km of total ascents and descents (with 8,478 ft being the tour's high point) as you pass in and out of the valleys that reach into three countries and define the massif's boundaries, valleys that attend the White Lady as if they were her courtiers.

Normally walked in an anti-clockwise direction over eleven days, a popular starting point is Les Houches, in France's Chamonix Valley, in Courmayeur in Italy's Aosta Valley, or near Martigny in Switzerland on the eastern boundary of the Rhone Valley. Wherever you decide to begin, this circuit of the 'Monarch of the Alps' – with its summit fully 3,700 m *above* the town of Chamonix – will be a highlight of your walking life. Most begin in Les Houches where you can take a cable car up to Bellevue with its panoramic outlook to Mont Blanc and the granite spires of the Aiguilles Rouges, before a steep ascent skirts the Bionnassay Glacier on the way to the Col du Tricot and past two charming alpine hamlets – Miage and Les Contamines-Montjoie. Leaving Les Contamines the real climbing begins, all the way to the Col du Bonhomme

Photo: Dominicus Johannes Bergsma

(7,641 ft). The Italian border is crossed at Col de la Seigne (8,255 ft) and here the views open to the horizons around you – the Val Veny ahead and the entire massif laid out to your left.

Descending past the Glacier du Miage and along the northern slopes of Mont Favre and down to Courmayeur, you'll want to get to bed early to prepare for the next day – a long climb to the tour's highlight – the grassy slopes of Mont de la Saxe and its views to the Mont Blanc range. More cols are crossed on the way down to Rifugio Bonatti, idyllically placed on a small grassy plateau opposite the Grandes Jorasses. Another stiff climb to Grand Col Ferret (8,323 ft) has you in Switzerland, and a long descent into the Val Ferret ends in the village of La Fouly. Next is an easy day's walking to Champex, situated in a saddle between two mountains, where two routes – one through woodlands but the other a higher rocky walk with a degree of difficulty – ends at Col de la Forclaz (5,010 ft) on the Chamonix–Martigny road, once little more than a track used by mule teams and smugglers.

Another steep climb – this time to the Col de Balme (6,991 ft) – ends in outstanding views to Mont Blanc that will continue as you move over the ridge of Aiguillette des Posettes (7,221 ft) and through the Aiguilles Rouges Nature Reserve (look for ibex and chamoix). You should consider an out-and-back diversion here to lovely Lac Blanc (7,717 ft) as you make your way to La Flegere and then above the Arve valley to the summit of Le Brevent (8,284 ft) and another fabulous Mont Blanc viewpoint. From Le Brevent take a cable car if you like down to Planpraz and Chamonix, past Refuge de Bellachat and through woodlands and forest ... and back to Les Houches.

The good news, too, is that because there is plentiful accommodation along the entire route it can be done in convenient sections if you're either pressed for time or lacking the necessary stamina. Make no mistake – should the weather turn nasty, and it will before you're done – the going will get tough, despite the trail's preponderance of 'easier' alternatives. And there is much more to this route than mountain peaks. Meadows, suspension bridges, the company one finds in its bric-a-brac-filled mountain 'refugios', bilberry, larch and alpenrose, and wildflowers – more than 2,500 species and subspecies of alpine flora. Something for everyone, as they say, or as one Swiss walker confessed recently: 'Many of us prefer the flowers to the summits'.

14. TRANS CANADA TRAIL
Canada

Distance: 23,000 km
Grade: Strenuous
Time: 2 years+

The Trans Canada Trail (TCT) was begun in 1992 on the 125th anniversary of Canada's founding and currently passes through almost 1,000 communities, providing a link for more than 34 million people. Eighty percent of Canada's population live less than 30 minutes from the TCT, and the aim is to have one vast, unbroken 23,000-km chain stretching across the nation and passing through every province and territory by 1 July 2017, Canada's 150th birthday. When finished, it will link the Arctic, Pacific and Atlantic oceans and will own the coveted title of the world's longest recreational trail, with its 'Mile Zero' in St John's,

Photo: Anthony DeLorenzo

Newfoundland and its western terminus in Victoria on Vancouver Island.

An ambitious project like this, built to encompass such a vast swathe of the North American continent, was always going to be more than just a single trail. It has two primary segments: the main section which runs through the towns and cities of heavily populated southern Canada and ending at its western terminus in Victoria, and a northern 'spur' which heads out from Alberta, passing through Edmonton and British Columbia and paralleling the Alaska Highway for about 1,000 km as it makes its way through the Yukon, the Northwest Territories and Nunavut. There is also an alternative water route here, using the Mackenzie River out of Great Slave Lake which will take you all the way to the Arctic Ocean and the town of Tuktoyaktuk, where the average winter temperature is minus 26 degrees Celsius. Or you can walk there too, along the banks of the Mackenzie River. Hardcore TCT-ers call it 'Walking the Tuk'. It is a Grand Adventure in itself.

In the east, Nova Scotia and New Brunswick are transforming hundreds of kilometres of disused rail lines into TCT trails, with Prince Edward Island's contribution being their very own Confederation Trail which spans the entire length of this crescent-shaped island. In Quebec two alternative trails will connect Quebec City to Montreal running either side of the St Lawrence Valley. Ontario will have around 4,000 km of the trail including a spur to Niagara, while 1,200 km of the trail will pass through southern Manitoba including a spur to Lake Winnipeg. The trail enters southern Saskatchewan and passes through its southern prairies through lovely Grasslands National Park and Duck Mountain Provincial Park before entering Alberta at Onion Lake. From there it follows Iron Horse Trail to

Edmonton where the northern spur as mentioned heads up through the Yukon while the southern route passes through the Rocky Mountains and into British Columbia.

The TCT is a testament to just what a well co-ordinated and dedicated grass roots volunteer programme can achieve when effectively combined with business groups and local and provincial government authorities. More than 125,000 Canadians have so far contributed – either by donations or actual trail building – to its construction. In excess of 400 trail sections are currently being managed and owned by various trail groups, conservation bodies and government agencies, with the bulk of it the result of the linking up of a veritable multitude of existing trails, such as the Kettle Valley Trail in British Columbia and the Galloping Goose Regional Trail on Vancouver Island. New sections are continuously being opened – and not to a little pomp and ceremony – everything from a tiny 1-km-long stretch through Trenton Park in Nova Scotia, opened in February 2015, to the Chief Whitecap Waterway in Saskatchewan, the province's first water trail officially opened in June 2015 and passing through Whitecap Dakota First Nation lands. Filling in all of the missing links in this mind-numbingly long chain will likely take trail builders right up to that July 2017 deadline.

If you intend to walk the entire trail as it is (something like 85 per cent completed) then you'd better spend some serious time preparing. I hope to walk a small section of it in southern Saskatchewan later this year, but that is nothing compared to the epic traverse of the trail made by the 39-year old Prince George forest technician Dana Meise, who set out from Cape Spear in Newfoundland in May 2008 and walked more than 16,000 km of the then heavily segmented trail, ending in Clover Point, Victoria, in December 2013. Along the way he learned how to fish for lobster, how to sail, found love in Thunder Bay, was beaten senseless by a hailstorm on an open prairie in Saskatchewan, woke up with a bear sniffing at his feet, and one day walked side by side with the wife of the Canadian prime minister. Meise became the first person to walk the British Columbia portion of the trail in its entirety from east to west. If you stay on any trail anywhere long enough, you're bound to accumulate some stories.

The TCT is a multi-use trail shared by hikers, cyclists, cross-country skiers, snow-mobiles, canoeists, kayakers and horseback riders, with regularly spaced shelters that provide both water and protection from the elements. The landscapes you can experience on it are as varied and idiosyncratic as Canada itself. Whether it's the 7-km gravelly wilderness of the abandoned Musquodoboit railway in Nova Scotia, or the Maukinak 'Path of the Paddle' water trail in northwestern Ontario that takes you along the northern shoreline of Saganaga Lake past 2.7-billion-year-old Precambrian cliffs and the 2-billion-year-old micro-fossils of Gunflint Lake. Whatever it is you are looking for, whatever you want to forget, or find, or whatever the challenge – the TCT will give you what you're looking for.

13. HAYDUKE TRAIL
Utah / Arizona, USA

Distance: 1,328 km
Grade: Strenuous
Time: 3 months

Is it a trail, or one of the most diabolical tests of endurance ever devised? The Hayduke Trail is 1,300 km of mostly backcountry hiking through the stunning red rock scenery of the Colorado Plateau, passing through some of America's most iconic national parks and the barren no-man's lands in between. The trail, however, is not one to take lightly. Its website even carries a warning that if you're not an experienced desert backpacker and in good physical condition then don't even think of walking so much as a section of it. It can thunderstorm, it can snow, water is scarce, and its winds can blow the ears off a donkey. But you don't walk the Hayduke Trail because it is easy. You come here because it is hard.

George Washington Hayduke III was a fictional character in the book *The Monkey Wrench Gang* (1975), written by the environmentalist Edward Paul Abbey (1927–1989). A tireless advocate for the preservation of America's wilderness, Abbey was an anarchist, an atheist, an opponent of laws relating to the public ownership of land, and despite working for a time for the National Parks Service he remained a fierce critic of how America's parks were managed. 'Every time you see a national forest sign that reads "Land of Many Uses"', he once said, 'just change that last word to "Abuses"'.

The book's four central characters – a Mormon river guide named Smith, the well-to-do surgeon Doc Sarvis, his impressionable female assistant Bonnie, and Hayduke himself – a former Green Beret – were 'eco-warriors', their lives dedicated to a common purpose: to oppose in any way they could the unchecked development of public lands in America's southwest. Hayduke's approach to wilderness, like his creator's, was uncompromising, raw, the real deal. Surely any trail that might come along one day with his fictional name attached to it would need to be something special too; a trail unlike any other.

It began humbly enough. Over 94 days in 1998, and again over 101 days in 2000, two avid Utah hikers – Mike Coronella and Joe Mitchell – backpacked their way through most of the vast Colorado Plateau's 'crown jewels' of parks: Arches National Park, Canyonlands National Park, Capitol Reef, Bryce Canyon, the Grand Staircase-Escalante and more. They blazed their way through National Forests, through designated Wilderness and Primitive areas, through isolated canyons and places like Poison Spring, past formations with names like Hole in the Rock, along Burr Trail and Willis Creek, Last Chance Creek and Dirty Devil River, around Horseshoe Mesa and down into the Grand Canyon itself, before exiting on to its North Rim and heading northwest to end it all in spectacular Zion National Park. Rarely did they take the easiest, or the most direct route, and everywhere they went they were conscious of the man who surely would have approved of their remarkable odyssey: Edward Abbey. Not long after completing their journey their call for the establishment of a thru-hike did not fall entirely on deaf ears, and was given impetus when Coronella and Mitchell's guidebook, *The Hayduke Trail: a Guide to the Backcountry Hiking Trail on the Colorado Plateau*, was published in 2005 by the University of Utah Press. And the rest, as they say, is history.

In the years following that second 'expedition', Mike and Joe refined the original route with help from the Southern Utah Wilderness Alliance, managing to keep it very much an informal path – the exact opposite of what you would find on other great American trails such as the Appalachian Trail or Pacific Crest Trail. On the Hayduke you had instead a series of 'suggested' routes over unmarked terrain, and now as if 1,300 km isn't long enough there are a series of optional 'diversions' that take you to places too numerous

Photo: Wolfgang Staudt

to mention here. Of course there are a number of 'known' pathways that the Hayduke takes because, after all, it is meant to be an uplifting visual and sensory experience and not merely a slog – paths like the Nankoweap Trail down from the Grand Canyon's North Rim, originally built by Major John Wesley Powell during his 1882 expedition so his geologist, Charles Walcott, could better see and catalogue the canyon's rock layers in the Supai Formation (285 million years old), the Redwall Limestone (average age 335 million years), and the rocks of the Muav Limestone (average age 515 million years). Hiking the Nankoweap is, like all Grand Canyon trails, a walk back in time. And a dangerous one, too. In fact the National Park Service named Nankoweap the canyon's most dangerous trail. Hardly surprising, then, that the Hayduke adopted it.

In the spirit of the fictional man after whom it is named, the Hayduke Trail runs entirely through public land. First thru-hiked by Brian Frankle in 2005 it has an impressive elevation range, from 550 m in the depths of the Grand Canyon to 3,480 m on the southern summit of Mount Ellen in Utah's Henry Mountains, the last mountain range in the Continental United States to be surveyed by the United States Geological Survey – over two vertical miles of elevation gain/loss, just another example of the trail's love of extremes, of its unrelenting isolation.

Each of its fourteen individual sections through the desert landscapes of southern Utah and northern Arizona is a test of endurance, stamina and resourcefulness, and to contemplate walking even just one means you need to be proficient with a compass and able to navigate your way around a topographical map (and take a GPS too). Keep your kit tight to minimise weight, and consider leaving the camera at home. Water purifier, inner soles, lightweight gaiters, flashlights and trekking poles are an absolute must, and carefully assemble your pack prior to leaving as only limited opportunities exist to buy missing items once you set out. You can walk for days here without seeing a water source (be careful not to drink any water from arsenic-tainted Rock Spring), and the next minute you could be hemmed in by flash flooding, courtesy of one of the region's ferocious thunderstorms.

To walk the whole thing right through, a feat managed by only a handful of hardy souls every year, will have you walking on every surface imaginable including slick rock, sandy washes, sand dunes, quicksand and scree. It intentionally does all it can to avoid towns and populated areas as it bisects regions under pressure from over-grazing and governmental mismanagement. Temperatures range from freezing to over 100 degrees Fahrenheit, and then there's the wildlife: coyotes, rattlesnakes, several species of scorpion. And mountain lions.

The Hayduke Trail is a 'rogue route', a path that even now with its growing reputation still manages to slip below the usual trail radar. To walk it is to see America the way Edward Abbey always believed it should be seen, crawling if necessary as he once famously said, 'on hands and knees, over the sandstone and through the thornbush and cactus. And when traces of blood begin to mark your trail, you'll see something, maybe'.

12. SOUTHWEST COASTAL PATH
Southwest England

Distance: 1,014 km
Grade: Moderate to Strenuous
Time: 5–8 weeks

The 1,014-km-long Southwest Coastal Path, the nation's longest national trail, begins at Minehead in Somerset and heads south, shadowing the well-worn trails of the coastguard – men whose job it was to clamp down on the rampant smuggling trade of the 18th and 19th centuries. The trails of the Southwest Coastal Path owe their meandering nature to these trails, trails that began being trampled into existence in the early 1800s after the establishment of the Coastguard Service in 1822 to rein in smugglers who had been bringing illegal goods into the country ever since the government slapped burdensome duties on to imported goods in the 1700s. The nature of their work meant the coastguard had to be able to peer down into a myriad of isolated and naturally sheltered coves and bays, which meant tracing pathways alongside some rather vertical cliffs – pathways that in many places are still followed today. Though long gone now, the coastguard's presence still echoes here as you pass by old stone stiles, the remains of dry stone walls, and the coast's smattering of repurposed coastguard cottages – accommodation that the coastguard were forced to build themselves as their presence was not welcomed by communities who were doing very nicely accommodating and feeding illegal smugglers.

Created in stages (there are 52 in total) with its final

segment between Somerset and North Devon opened in 1978, it is now widely held to be England's finest coastal path, and is one of the world's must-do walks. The path is mostly, though for no particular reason, walked in an anti-clockwise direction, beginning in Minehead. The very fit can do it in four weeks (although bear in mind its approximate total elevation gain is somewhere between three and four times the height of Mount Everest). If this is your first time, however, then you're going to want to take it much slower than that. A natural history showcase of uplifted, eroded coastlines, the jewel in its crown is the Jurassic Coast in Dorset and East Devon, England's first natural World Heritage Site which provides a window on 185 million years of earth's geological history. And there is significant human history here too, with areas that have been inhabited since Neolithic times when dense inland forests forced hunter-gathering communities to live along more open coastal fringes.

The varied nature of this trail becomes evident south of Somerset as you enter Exmoor National Park, an upland expanse of open moorland with its coastal heaths a Site of Special Scientific Interest, before linking with the Coleridge Way which takes you through a series of sites connected to the poet Samuel Coleridge (1772–1834). There is so much ahead of you at this point it defies summarising. In North Devon there's Great Hangman, the path's high point at 318 m and the highest sea cliff in England; in North Cornwall the remains of Tintagel and its castle with its mythic connections to King Arthur and Camelot; in West Cornwall there is the gorgeous sweep of St Ives Bay; and then Land's End, England's most westerly landmass – before skirting Lizard Point on the Lizard Peninsula, Great Britain's most southerly point, as you turn northwards in the direction of bustling Falmouth.

Plymouth and Dartmouth provide plenty of great accom-

Photo: Dietrich Krieger

modation options before a crossing of the River Dart takes you into the 'English Riviera' through the coastal towns of Goodrington, Paignton and Torquay, birthplace of novelist Agatha Christie. The path melds with the South Devon Railway sea wall from Dawlish Warren to Dawlish and again along the promenade at Teignmouth, then once through Exmouth the climb begins to the High Land of Orcombe, the start of the walk's most spectacular stretch along the Jurassic Coast. The assemblage of Triassic, Jurassic and Cretaceous cliffs provides an almost complete record of the Mesozoic Era (252 to 66 million years ago), and there are plenty of natural wonders besides such as the limestone arch of Durdle Door at the end of the 120-m isthmus that connects it to the mainland. The path runs along the entire length of the Jurassic Coast, which is where you need to pause and take one of the many guided walks that lead you among its eroded rock formations and provide insights into ancient habitats, and ecosystems long-since vanished.

A host of charming villages lie ahead of you, including the sloping cobbled streets of Lyme Regis, the fishing hamlet of Seatown, Abbotsbury with its lovely 14th-century St Catherine's Chapel, and the Georgian and Regency-style houses that line the seafront of Weymouth, much-visited by George III. There is the 144-million-year old fossil forest near Lulworth Cove, the gorgeous murals at Swanage painted by local artist Nina Camplin, and finally a walk across Studland Beach to Poole Harbour, having completed a rollercoaster ride of clifftops and hidden coves, of tin mines and forested subtropical creeks, a UNESCO Biosphere Reserve and five Areas of Outstanding Natural Beauty – a walk with a surprise around every corner.

11. ALTA VIA 1
Trentino Alto Adige, Italy

Distance: 119 km
Grade: Moderate
Time: 11 days

The French geologist Deodat de Dolomieu travelled to the Dolomites in 1788, and was the first to identify the calcium magnesium carbonate (dolomite) and calcium carbonate (calcite) which together compose these *Monti Pallidi*, the so-called 'Pale Mounts' which we now call the Dolomites in his honour. Or if the science of their colour seems a little dry, why not try the myth – that these pale mountains were once covered in the finest strands of gossamer which spread out and became infused with a beguiling mix of pinkish-orange hues, a tapestry born in moonbeams for a beautiful princess bride in a wonderland of pinnacles, peaks and towers.

These pale mountains, the most 'hikeable' on the planet, bring out the poet in us all. They even captured the heart of Reinhold Messner, the world's most famous mountaineer, who called them, simply, 'the most beautiful mountains in the world'. But they are mountains that possess a bewildering array of possible trails, and it can be difficult to know where to start. What makes that decision a little easier, however, are the six Alta Via (High Route) trails each of which takes a medium to high altitude and bisects these mountains in a series of north-south lines, varying in length from six days to two weeks, and varying also in difficulty, with routes to suit both novice ramblers and rope-assisted junkies. Alta Via 1 and 2 are the more accessible, with routes 3 to 6 passing through wilder, less populated ranges.

Photo: Patafisik

The Alta Via 1 is the 'must-do' trail for the first-time multi-day hiker. A point-to-point trail with clearly defined segments, it passes through the Dolomites' heart and gets you in among its best-known peaks such as Tofana di Rozes (10,581 ft/3,225 m), Lagazuoi (9,301 ft/2,835 m), Monte Pelmo (10,393 ft/3,168 m), and Monte Civetta (10,560 ft/3,220 m) with its magnificent 3-km-long vertical northwest face, a symbol of the Dolmites that rises to a dizzying 1,200 m. There is no glacier walking or rock climbing involved on Alta Via 1, though there are several sections of rocky and steep ground. Trails are solid and wide with minimal elevation gain/loss, and if you like alpine flowers – and the Dolomites have more than 1,500 species of them – then the best month to go is July, while fauna sightings will invariably include marmots, roe and red deer, chamois and ibex.

Normally walked from north to south, the trail begins at Lago di Braies and after an initial stiff climb to Rifugio Biella (7,545 ft/2,300 m) the trail maintains a gentler gradient as you pass Malga Fanes Grande (6,896 ft/2,102 m). Turning east after reaching Rifugio Lagazuoi you can detour to see a tunnel built by the Italians to attack Austro-Hungarian troops on Lagazuoi summit during World War I. The Dolomites became an unlikely battlefield in that conflict, and mule tracks that were cut into what was the war's most forbidding theatre complemented the many ancient shepherd's paths that are today such a vital part of the Alta Via's trail network.

A rest day should be had in lovely Cortina, a worthwhile detour down into the Ampezzo Valley if only to see the wonderful Rinaldo Zardini Palaeontology Museum with its hundreds of local fossils that remind us the Dolomites were once at the bottom of a vast tropical sea. Back on the Alta Via you now walk to Rifugio Nuvolau (8,448 ft/2,575

m) with its stunning views and more optional routes to the Cinque Torri (Five Towers) above Cortina. An assortment of cables and ladders aid your descent from the *rifugio* on to a wide, grassy plain before descending into woodlands and yet another detour. This time it is the fabulous Monte Pelmo Circuit, a 42-km loop around Monte Pelmo with its beautiful, arc-like glacial cirque – what the English-born 19th-century author and mountaineer John Ball once called 'a gigantic fortress of the most massive architecture' – that can be done in four days.

Rounding Monte Civetta you reach Paso Duran (5,252 ft/1,601 m) over gentle terrain and a good path through remote hills leads to another *rifugio* before the final serious ascent of the trail takes you to a col beneath the summit of Cime de Zita, before your final night at yet another spectacularly sited *rifugio* ahead of the final descent through woodlands to La Pissa – and buses to take you to your final destination of Belluno.

The wonder of the Dolomites lies not just in its pinnacles or in the hues of its minerals, but in the very way these mountains are dispersed. Unlike so many of Europe's Alps they are not laid down in parallel valleys with adjoining ridge lines, but are instead a collection of mountain groups most of which are independent from those about them, mountains that seem to have been randomly scattered across the northern Italian landscape – a randomness that allows for literally hundreds of inter-connecting trails that can have you returning here every year for the rest of your life, each time discovering something new in the world's most mesmerising calcium carbonate-laden terrain.

10. BUCKSKIN GULCH
Utah, USA

Distance: 21 km
Grade: Easy to Moderate
Time: 1–2 days

Deep within the remote 112,500-acre Paria Canyon–
Vermilion Cliffs Wilderness, almost hidden from sight
on the Utah side of the Utah/Arizona border, Buckskin
Gulch is the slot canyon every lover of slot canyons longs to
conquer. 'Your list of slot canyons is incomplete until you've
come here', they'll tell you, and it's no good arguing the
point. Buckskin Gulch is the longest, deepest slot canyon in
the southwest and while not perhaps the prettiest (its rocks
lack some of the light and colour of other slot canyons) it is
nevertheless unrivalled in its variety of terrain: it is replete
with fluted rock walls of Navajo sandstone, and the Chinle
and Moenave formations make up many sections. With most
of its tortuous course less than 3 m wide, there are some
bottlenecks so narrow you'll be removing your pack in order
to squeeze your way through.

How much of Buckskin Gulch you see and experience will
depend upon how much time you have and which of its four
trailheads you approach it from. The vast majority of hikers
choose to do it in a day, and to do this you need to start at
the Wire Pass Trailhead, located about 13 km south of US89
on House Rock Valley Road and from which it's about 2.6
km to its confluence with Buckskin Gulch. Taking this route
allows you to bypass the upper 6.5 km of the canyon, which
is not its most dramatic stretch. Immersing yourself in Wire

Pass is a lovely teaser, a short drainage passage into Buckskin with walls nowhere as high as those yet to come, but walking it is like threading the eye of a needle at times, plus you can take some lovely photographs of its illuminated walls that can – depending upon the sun's position – be lit all the way to the canyon floor. But it is when you emerge into Buckskin itself that the real fun begins.

Buckskin Gulch is a tributary of the Paria River, and can be a dangerous place when it rains: water drains from countless streams across the Paria Plateau into the river and in no time is funnelled through its crevasses and sandy bottom like a fury, washing everything before it. This is why the most popular time to hike it is the dry period from April to June, when flash flooding is less likely to occur. Permits can easily be picked up at its trailheads if you decide you're up to doing it from Wire Pass in one long day, although two days is a much more 'civilised' and rewarding option. Unfortunately, to stay overnight you will require an overnight permit – these are often snapped up as much as six months in advance, so plan well ahead. However, don't let the paperwork dissuade you. It's worth a little advance preparation to traverse this multi-hued wonder of nature.

Buckskin Gulch is no walk in the park. It involves rock scrambling, and you're going to get your feet wet, too, although the depth of any water encountered is rarely above 1 m – flood waters notwithstanding. And obstacles include a beautifully wedged boulder in Wire Pass and various other rock jams that will require a little rope work (about 6 m should do it) to get your pack up and over. You'll want boots here too, not Nikes. Almost a quarter of all recreational injuries in the United States are sprains, and this is just the sort of place you're likely to get one. You'll also want to bring a topographical map with you and know how to read

Photo: John Fowler

it. GPSs are ok at either end of the canyon but once you're inside and direct lines to the sky above become intermittent thanks to the 160-m-high walls that surround you, well, they just will not work through rock. Sandy bottoms can be transformed into 20-ft-deep pools of swirling frothing water in mere minutes. And for most of its length the walls are so high any thought of getting up and out should the weather unexpectedly turn horrible is, well, a forlorn hope. No wonder, then, that this trail regularly makes the list of the United States' most dangerous hikes.

Although you'll encounter residual pools of muddy water and the aforementioned streams, there will be no drinkable water sources so be sure to bring enough water with you. The terrain, though, is forgiving – a mixture of sand and stones/boulders that present no technical difficulties but might result in your progress not being quite what one would expect over what is essentially a flat, gradient-free trail. Along the way you'll encounter sandbanks with grasses, trees and wildflowers, as well as boulders, tree stumps and log jams that are never in the same place twice, which makes Buckskin Gulch a different experience each time, no matter how many times you come here.

Buckskin Gulch is a beguiling crack in the fabric of the Colorado Plateau, isolated enough (mercifully) from the tourist hotspots around it – the Grand Canyon to the south and most of Grand Staircase–Escalante National Monument above and around it – to ensure you'll have an experience to remember deep within one of America's most spectacular hidden treasures.

9. CINQUE TERRE CLASSIC
Liguria, Italy

Distance: 12 km
Grade: Easy
Time: Half a day

I can still remember the sound he made as he fell. My wife Yvonne and I were in northern Italy walking a meandering piece of the Cinque Terre Classic trail high above the warm waters of the Ligurian Sea, following the fence line along the perimeter of a centuries-old farm on a path that was really more of a goat track than a trail. It was then that a man raced past us only to lose his footing a few metres on before tripping and falling in a tangle of limbs down the hillside, coming to rest with a thud against the trunk of an olive tree. He screamed in pain, and as his friends came to his aid and placed each of his arms around their shoulders, lifting the weight off what was a severely sprained ankle, all I could think of as I stood there unsympathetically was: 'Now why would you want to rush a walk like this?' The Cinque Terre is a fragile landscape, susceptible to slippage and erosion after heavy rains, which means you need to watch your footing even when the sun is shining. The views are of course a welcome distraction, but can be an occupational hazard, too. On a clear day, you can see as far as Corsica.

People have been living here long before the earliest historical records dating from the 11th century came down to us, and the trail you see now is not unlike all those that went before it and are still here in various states of repair, used by generations of farming families who have waged

Photo: Thomas Shahan

long battles with a hard soil to make it and keep it fertile. It is a land of terraces – an astonishing 7,000 km of dry stone walls if they were all laid end to end – a complex assemblage providing precious level ground for grape vines and olive trees and a bounty that sun-drenched, south-facing Italian hillsides are so adept at producing.

These days the trail we call the Cinque Terre joins five villages along a dramatic 16-km-long portion of this sloping coastline. The villages of Monterosso al Mare, Vernazza, Corniglia, Manarola and Riomaggiore are the embodiment of what you come to expect from rural Italy, all full of colour and shuttered windows, its buildings almost Dali-esque in the way they lean ever so slightly so that one almost seems to prop up another beside it. The villages of the Cinque Terre are blissfully automobile-free, and the most time it will take you to walk from one to the other is less than two hours, which makes for a delightfully segmented day's walking. And they are accessible too, thanks to a nearby train line that passes through them all, making it easy to begin your walk from whichever village most takes your fancy, so you can walk as much or as little of the trail as you like.

The trails that once spread around them like a spider's web were not built for recreational purposes but to link working farms and communities, to provide pilgrims who came here to worship with access to hillside sanctuaries, or donkeys with a path to transport produce. Land here is at a premium, and nothing is wasted. Herb gardens, garlic, chestnut trees, oranges, lemons – even wild asparagus – have been grown here for generations. As you walk by you are so close to them it's hard to resist the temptation to reach out and grab yourself an impromptu snack.

Though there is more than one path, the most popular, the one which nine out of ten visitors here take, is the coastal

Sentiero Azzurro, the famous 'Blue Path' (there is also the *Sentiero del Crinale,* the 'High Path' which is three times the length of the Blue Path and follows a route that is slightly more inland, and therefore not as popular as its coast-hugging cousin). My wife and I, like most, began in Riomaggiore, the easternmost of the five villages that quickly had us on what is probably the trail's most famous stretch, the *Via dell' Amore,* the 'Street of Love', constructed in the late 1920s to provide access to a tunnel on the Genoa to La Spezia rail line. The second village, Manarola, is reached after walking barely 1 km, easily the shortest of the four sections. From Manarola it is 2 km to Corniglia, the village least affected by tourism because it's the only one of the five that is set well back from the ocean. On the way to Corniglia you'll need to climb the 33 flights and 382 steps of the Lardarina stairway, which take you up to the plaza Largo Taragio. From the plaza we climbed a further two sets of staircases to the ruined remains of an old Genoese fort and sat in the shade looking down the coast back towards Manarola.

The 3.2 km from Corniglia to Vernazza, one of the most beautiful villages in all Liguria and the most 'medieval' of the five, takes you higher still, through forests and and over promontories with stunning views out over the Cinque Terre Riviera before your descent into a village that tumbles its way down to the water's edge and is impossible to walk through without stopping, with its many cafes and restaurants providing views over its tiny port. It's also worth visiting the remains of the Castillo dei Doria, built to protect the town from invading Saracens. The last section, just over 3 km to Monterosso al Mare, involves a climb of around 150 m from Vernazza's port and opens up to some of the trail's finest panoramas with views back down to Vernazza. This final section, which will have you crossing several old bridges and passing under evergreen oaks and junipers, will take you a couple of hours. But the advantage of walking the Cinque Terre east to west is that you can end your day soaking up the sun on Monterosso al Mare's Fegina Beach, a *sand* beach – a rarity for this part of Italy – and once named by *Forbes* magazine as one of the world's 'sexiest' beaches.

Unlike other coastal trails that can involve a lot of 'up and down', the Cinque Terre's Blue Path is remarkably flattish, maintaining a more or less constant elevation with the only real exceptions being the descents to its villages. And while the distances involved might suggest it takes around four hours to traverse, a full day should be its bare minimum. And two days? Even better.

8. TROTTERNISH RIDGE
Isle of Skye, Scotland

Distance: 37 km
Grade: Moderate
Time: 2 days

A challenging trail on the largest and northernmost island of the Inner Hebrides, this walk along the Isle of Skye's Trotternish Ridge begins in Flodigarry, a small settlement on the eastern side of the Trotternish Peninsula and continues south to The Storr, a craggy summit overlooking the Sound of Raasay. The trail runs through a landscape born of a series of landslips so massive it even has its own geological term – the Quiraing, Great Britain's longest geological landslip. On the way the wealth of natural sights you'll see as you clamber across this outlandish realm, this pulsating, living landscape, are predictably impressive: the pinnacle that is the Old Man of Storr high above Loch Leathan; the 37-m-high Needle; the pyramidal rocky peak called The Prison. And while you don't need to know how all these landforms came to exist in order to appreciate their beauty, knowing precisely how this misshapen world got here will lift the experience of walking one of the nation's most spectacular ridge walks still higher, maybe even into the realm of 'life-changing'.

Looking at it all you inevitably wonder: 'How did it happen?' Like most good things: slowly. Sixty million years ago Jurassic sediments – sandstones and clays, though mostly shale – were laid down and later overlaid by dozens of thick Tertiary basalt lava flows. No longer able to bear the accumulated weight pressing down upon it, the sediments began to be turned sideways on a north-south trending fault, its rocks dipping almost uniformly to the west, as if in homage to the setting sun. A process that produced a multi-level, step-like and angular landscape. Dolerite sills and dykes then intruded to add further complications. The landslips – the largest in Europe's history – produced the steep scarp slopes you see on its eastern fringes. The last Ice Age then intervened, compressing the ridge and grinding away at its stacks and pinnacles to give us the conglomeration of shapes and tsunami waves of upswept rock we see today.

For the majority of the trail there is no designated path. And it can be surprisingly easy to get lost once you leave the familiar points of reference behind. It can be dangerous. Walking here takes you by angular inclines of volcanic rock and along near-vertical cliffs. And although you won't see it with the naked eye, the land here is still moving. Every year the road out of Flodigarry crawls with repair vehicles fixing the cracks in its buckled surfaces. The landscape does not

Photo: arjecahn

conform to any typical 'ridge and mountain' outline. When Hollywood film director Ridley Scott wanted an alien world to act as a backdrop for his science-fiction epic *Prometheus*, he came here.

The 'Old Man of Storr' may well be one of the most photographed landforms in Great Britain, but it is just the teaser. It is the ridge itself that best defines this twisted, restless peninsula, and the best way to reach it is by taking the footpath from Flodigarry to Loch Langaig and on to Loch Hasco, then climb till you're below the crags of the Quiraing. Once there, scramble towards the top till you reach a high point overlooking The Needle, The Prison and The Table – an elevated plateau of short grass legends say was once used to hide cattle from invading Vikings. From above The Table you descend to the southwest then climb to the summit of Bioda Buidhe (466 m) which will provide a wonderful view down over the spectacular winding road through the Quiraing and may also provide views as far as Staffin Bay if the weather is clear. After a further descent you then climb to Bealach (narrow mountain pass) Uige, after which the ridge narrows appreciably before crossing over a series of gentle summits and down to another *bealach* with a number of sheltered camp sites.

The next summit is Beinn Edra (611 m), with 360-degree views south to the rawness of the Cuillin Massif, formed by intrusions of igneous rock called 'plutons'; west to the flat-topped hills of MacLeod's Tables; north to the Isle of Harris and Lewis, Scotland's largest island and the third-largest island in the British Isles; and east to the mountains of Torridon.

Then you're climbing again, this time to Sgurr a'Mhadaidh Ruaidh, the 'Red Fox' summit with wonderful views down to Loch Cuithir. Hugging the very edge of the escarpment you then ascend to the summit of Baca Ruadh and move along what is now an increasingly undulating ridge before descending to Bealach Hartaval where a short but steep ascent will put you on Hartaval's 669-m summit.

It's then down again to Bealach a'Chuirn (a possible camp site with water) from where a long climb over a broad slope will deposit you on the 719-m summit of The Storr, the walk's high point where you can gaze down upon the Storr Sanctuary's rock pinnacles which include, of course, the Old Man of Storr. Descending now to Bealach Beag means the best of the ridge is now behind you, and you have a choice: either depart the ridge and make for the car park, or continue along a final angst-inducing ascent before a line of bogs signals your approach to Portree, Skye's main town set around a lovely natural harbour fringed by a network of hills and cliffs and home to a wide choice of hotels and B&Bs, any of which make an excellent place to stop and pause, to give yourself time to consider the wondrous landscapes you've left behind.

7. BRIGHT ANGEL TRAIL / SOUTH KAIBAB TRAIL CIRCUIT
Grand Canyon, Arizona, USA

Distance: 27.3 km
Grade: Strenuous
Time: 2 days

The first thing that crosses the mind of many a part-time hiker arriving at the Bright Angel Trail trailhead on the

Photo: Don Graham

South Rim of Arizona's Grand Canyon is the assumption that they have aimed too high, that the gaping chasm beneath them will swallow them whole should they enter it, and that even if they succeed in making it unscathed to the canyon floor, the walk back up will somehow do them in. And that's the moment when you have to start thinking with your head, to remind yourself of all the research you did that brought you here, all of the physical preparation, and know that if you just keep in mind a very few basic statistics relating to two of America's greatest trails, you can do this. It is a 4,380-ft descent from where you are standing down to the banks of the Colorado River, just 2.5 km to the first resthouse, and 2.4 km to the one after that. Going down, everyone will tell you, is actually surprisingly easy. It's the 'getting back up' you need to think about.

Bright Angel Trail is a maintained dirt trail with an average 10 per cent gradient along its entire length. It has been the most popular path down into the canyon from the South Rim ever since the Havasupai people first built the upper reaches of it centuries ago so they could access fresh water at Garden Creek, a technical canyon (meaning some rock-climbing skills will be needed to ascend and descend) a mile down from the popular rest stop of Indian Gardens. A US Senator, Ralph Cameron, improved the trail all the way to the canyon floor after coming to live on the canyon rim in 1890, which is why – for a few years at least – it was known as the Cameron Trail.

It descends from the rim along the head of a side canyon and almost immediately you are negotiating a seemingly endless series of switchbacks beneath towering cliffs as you make your way to Mile-and-a-Half Resthouse (toilets), and Three-Mile Resthouse (no toilets). The trail flattens out as you approach Indian Garden, then crosses the tough

Tapeats sandstone of the desolate Tonto Platform, one of the canyon's most impressive geological features, before following a cottonwood-filled gully to where Pipe Creek joins with the Colorado River. You have now descended almost a vertical mile from the trailhead above, and have been hiking for between four and five hours. It's now only a half-hour walk to Silver Bridge over the Colorado River to Bright Angel Campground about a third of a mile downstream from Phantom Ranch, the canyon floor's only lodging (bookings essential!), a beautiful mosaic of rough-hewn timbers and native stone constructed in 1922 and designed by the American architect Mary Colter.

Presuming you take the cheaper option and pitch a tent, you'll waken at Bright Angel Campground early the next morning to be confronted with a choice you will have already made: do you climb back to the rim on the trail you just came down on, or do you take the South Kaibab Trail, which will return you to the rim to the east of the Bright Angel trailhead near the Visitor's Center. Taking the South Kaibab Trail means you won't be looking at the same views twice, but there is no water available and it is far more open than the more shaded Bright Angel Trail, though this openness means it is virtually free from snow, making it a year-round option. Unlike other canyon trails the South Kaibab was designed to take the most direct route to the bottom on a smooth, 4-ft-wide path that passes by the Vishnu schist of the inner gorge before going on to encounter no fewer than eight major geological formations alongside of which an exciting series of switchbacks drilled and blasted into vertical cliffs take you past the Toroweap Foundation, Coconino Sandstone, and the fine-grained, thin-bedded siltstone of the Hermit Formation and up to its trailhead at Yaki Point, back on the canyon's South Rim.

While the Bright Angel/South Kaibab option is eminently doable with an overnight stay at Bright Angel Campground, even for a fit part-time hiker, there are several things all of us need to keep in mind before setting out. Remember to wet your hat and shirt, as this will reduce your body temperature. Take trekking poles, drink plenty of water, and eat high-energy snack foods – even if you're not hungry. Take a 15-minute break for every hour you walk, try to elevate your legs when you stop to avoid a build-up of lactic acid, and if walking in a group always allow the weakest walker to set the pace. Don't attempt to walk down and out of the canyon in the same day, especially in the warmer months from May to September, and never hike back up in the mid-afternoon heat, if only to avoid the lower elevations with their walls of dark grey schist that radiates the heat of the afternoon sun the way a cast-iron stove throws off the heat of a roaring fire. More than 250 people are rescued from the Grand Canyon every year. Don't become one of them!

6. MILFORD TRACK
Southland, New Zealand

Distance: 53.5 km
Grade: Moderate
Time: 4 days

Blanche Baugham was born in Surrey, England, in 1870, the youngest of six children. She gained a BA in Classical Literature, became involved in the suffrage movement, and in 1900 travelled to New Zealand where she pursued her interest in poetry. In 1908, after having been published regularly in the London *Spectator*, she travelled to Milford Sound, and walked the Milford Track. Baugham later wrote an essay on her experience, titling it 'The Finest Walk in the World'. It's a title still used today. Why? Because this walk has all the ingredients necessary to be the world's finest. The rest just depends on how well you argue it.

Milford Sound, crowned by majestic Mitre Peak which rises 1,692 m above its placid waters, is on the southwest coast of New Zealand's South Island in the region of 'Fiordland', one of New Zealand's last places to be mapped. Formed by tectonic activity over millions of years that built up mountains which were then pushed aside by the glaciers that had expanded to fill its valleys (technically making it a 'fiord', not a 'sound'), it measures 16 km from the head of the fiord to where it opens into the Tasman Sea. During the last Ice Age the glaciers began to melt, gouging out the valleys and displacing the boulders you can still see today as you pass through the Eglington Valley either in your own car or on a pre-booked bus from Queenstown to Te Anau Downs (the bus is a more practical option, as the walk is strictly one-way). At Te Anau Downs a twice-daily boat service or on-demand water taxis will then take you to your starting point at Glade Wharf on the shores of Lake Te Anau – and into a world of temperate rainforests, waterfalls, lichens and a blanket of dense greenery fed by an annual rainfall totalling almost 7 m and where downpours of less than an inch an hour are dismissed by locals as 'mist'. It is officially the country's wettest inhabited place, with a rate of precipitation that led *The New York Times* to dub it 'New Zealand's Watery Wild'.

The Milford Track, part of the Te Wahipounamu UNESCO World Heritage Site, leaves Glade Wharf and immediately

Photo: Alasdair W

immerses you in a beautiful forest of beech as you walk the banks of the Clinton River to Clinton Hut, a short 90-minute walk that leaves plenty of time to explore nearby swimming holes and takes the boardwalk through the surrounding wetlands and their understorey dominated by ferns, mosses, lichens and woody plants. A 16.5-km walk on Day 2 has you ascending along the trout-filled Clinton River through grassy meadows and past swamp pools before ascending to the river's source at Lake Mintaro in the shadows of Mackinnon Pass (3,520 ft), the track's high point. The walls of rock that tower above you on the approach to the pass are nothing short of inspiring as you move through the Clinton Valley and continue climbing towards your accommodation at Mintaro Hut, the landscape changing from temperate rainforest to a world of sub-alpine scrub, tussocks, and alpine herbs. Note: if the weather is fine you should continue on the 500-m climb up the head of the valley to Mackinnon Pass for the panoramic mountain views, because you never know what the next day's weather will bring. After contemplating the view from Twelve Second Rock – that's how long it would take for you to hit the ground if you fell off it – head back down to Mintaro Hut.

A preponderance of rocks and tree roots can make the 950-m descent from Mackinnon Pass down into the Arthur Valley difficult on Day 3, and is generally considered to be the most challenging part of the track. But the views you have more than compensate for that – from the monstrously sheer walls of the west face of the pass down into the moss-laden forests of Clinton Canyon and down past the cascades of Roaring Burn. Immersed again in beech forests the sound of an approaching waterfall soon becomes a roar as you pass by the base of mighty Sutherland Falls, at 1,904 ft New Zealand's highest waterfall, and on to your bed for the night at Dumpling

Hut. An early start the next morning is needed to make sure you cover the final 18 km – along the Arthur River and the blue-green waters of MacKay Creek, and around Ada Lake to a grand view of Giant's Gate Falls – to make the 2.00pm boat from Sandfly Point to the small settlement of Milford Sound, and the end of a memorable journey.

Numbers on this fragile trail are strictly regulated, and each of the three huts along the track must be booked and paid for in advance during the walking season which runs from late October to late April (the track is open May to September, but with reduced facilities, though it can then be walked both ways). All huts have 40 bunks with mattresses, water, flushing toilets, basins, heating, and cooking facilities, but there are no cooking utensils or showers. A maximum of 40 independent walkers are allowed to depart Glade Wharf each day, and camping along the track is not permitted. There are also three private lodges for use by guided walkers only, as well as four day shelters, and your itinerary must be iron-clad in order to maintain the carefully crafted ratio of bums to beds – so no skipping huts allowed!

The Milford Track is a designated 'Great Walk', meaning its trails are of a high standard, are well formed, and simple to follow – torrential downpours notwithstanding. If you're an experienced 'tramper' and the weather is good, you'll likely not consider it a particularly challenging experience. But the fact is that rain is likely, and even in summer there can be snow on its higher elevations. But you want the rain here, at least for a day, because when it rains a thousand waterfalls emerge all about you like silvery threads. And while heavy downpours can result in detouring to higher ground, the rain is a necessary ingredient here otherwise the track would not be what many say that it is – the finest walk in the world.

5. INCA TRAIL
Arequipa, Peru

Distance: 45 km
Grade: Moderate
Time: 4 days

This extraordinary trail, which routinely tops travellers' lists as their most unforgettable adventure, begins two hours out of the Peruvian city of Cuzco, a city redesigned in the 15th century, prior to the arrival of the Spanish, over a pre-Inca settlement during the rule of Pachacuti, to become the capital of the *Tawantinsuyu* Inca Empire. With its harmonic blend of Incan and Spanish conquistador-era architecture Cuzco is worth exploring over two or three days, if only to assist in acclimatising to the high altitudes to come as you prepare yourself for your journey into the Sacred Valley and the magical 'Lost City' of Machu Picchu, perched as dramatically as any city or dwelling in the world is perched – on a narrow ridge between Machu Picchu Mountain and Huayna Mountain, 2,450 m above the Urubamba River below.

Day 1 begins at the Km 82 road marker a bus ride out of Cuzco at an elevation of 2,800 m on the banks of the Urubamba. From there you walk 14 km on a gentle ascent along the Cusichaca Valley that will take you past the pre-Inca semi-circle-shaped settlement of Patallaqta at the confluence of the Willkanuta and Kusichaka Rivers which you'll see only from the trail as most tours don't include a diversion to this interesting site that would have been home to over a thousand people at the height of the Inca Empire. From here the trail connects with the Mollepata Trail (3,000

m) at the village of Wayllapampa, the last inhabited village on the route and the point where many consider the 'real' trail begins. From here you turn westward and follow a tributary of the Kusichaka, at which point all animals and even metal-tipped trekking poles are left behind to prevent trail erosion. It's worth pushing on to Ayapata Campground, because the second day is the longest and hardest, and camping a little ahead of other more frequented campgrounds provides a welcome head start.

On Day 2 the scenery becomes increasingly breathtaking as you climb the Llullucha Valley and make for the trail's highest point at Warmi Wanusqa, 'Dead Woman's Pass' (4,215 m). On the way you will pass groves of rare Polylepis trees, gnarled shrubs that belong to the rose family, which are wind-pollinated and endemic to the mid and high elevations of the tropical Andes, making it the world's highest flowering genus – so not to be walked past as though they are mere shrubs! An expanse of treeless grasslands – the Puna – follows, and an open slope with in-your-face views of nearby mountain crags sees you on Dead Woman's Pass with its sweeping views of the Huayanay Massif, before descending some 600 m on a steep gradient to Pakaymayu, and your camp for the night.

Early on Day 3 you climb again, this time on an ancient Inca stairway to the substantial remains of Runkuracay – either built as a lookout or perhaps as a tambo, a wayside stop for couriers complete with sleeping accommodation and stables for their horses. The trail leads on to its second pass at Abra de Runkuracay (3,500 m) and then descends into a valley with a small lake where the path changes from dirt to stone – the start of the very same route once trodden by the Incas themselves. Sayacmarca, a fort perched on a rocky spur overlooking the valley, is next, accessed via a narrow

Photo: Colegota

stone stairway with a steep drop-off on the right-hand side to the rocks below. Another descent follows, this time down to a causeway that may once have crossed a small lake, before climbing again and passing through a delightful piece of Inca engineering – an 8-m-long tunnel that was cut from a natural fissure in the rock and made big enough for the passage of men, animals and supplies.

Climbing still further you reach the third pass at Phuyupatamarca (Cloud-level Town), a place of ritual with a series of fountains and terraced baths – the higher baths reserved for use by Inca nobility, and the baths below for the lower classes who had to bathe in the nobility's discarded waters. Below Phuyupatamarca the trail twists steeply down into genuine jungle on an irregular Inca staircase that provides views over the Willkanuta River as you descend (while listening for the sound of trains running along the valley floor!) to Winay Wayna (Forever Young), named after a local pink orchid. Winay Wayna's marvellous collection of baths used for ritualistic cleansing and its array of agricultural terraces would make it worthy of a stop, even without its often overcrowded Trekkers' Hostel, and it is the trail's last official campsite.

Day 4 begins, and the start of the trail's final section – 3 km of mercifully easy and flat ground ending in a short, steep staircase which delivers you to Intipunku, the famed Gateway of the Sun, through the rectangular doorway of which you can at last gaze upon the remains of Machu Picchu before starting on the short path down to the famed city, built as a royal retreat for the Inca emperor Pachacuti around 1450 only to be abandoned a century later during the Spanish conquest – and remaining hidden from the outside world until its rediscovery in 1911 by the American explorer and academic Hiram Bingham.

The trail to Machu Picchu can be hiked over as little as two days, or as many as five. The two-day option means taking a bus for a 2.5-hour ride to the village of Chachabamba at the Km 104 road marker, thus getting a significant jump on those who begin at the traditional Km 82 marker. A four-hour hike to Winay Wayna follows before continuing on to the Sun Gate for those unforgettable views over the city itself.

4. ANNAPURNA CIRCUIT
Annapurna Massif, Nepal

Distance: 190 km
Grade: Strenuous
Time: 2–3 weeks

You can stand on the shoreline of Phewa Lake in the town of Pokhara in central Nepal and see them reflected in its still waters – Machapuchare (22,943 ft/6,993 m) and the other peaks of the eastern Annapurna Massif – a gigantic wall of white that glistens and sparkles anew every morning. It is an overwhelming sight, looking at 20,000 ft-plus summits from a lake that is not only a mere 2,434 ft/742 m above sea level, but a scant 28 km away! Add to that the Himalayas' forested foothills, populated by the nation's highest level of ethnic diversity, and you have an experience before you that rewards in ways far beyond that of mere topography.

The Annapurna Circuit is the classic of classic walks, three weeks on a giant loop on 190 km of trails that begin to the east of Pokhara in the town of Besisahar, where you'll mingle with tourists who come here in everything from luxurious private carriers, taxis, public buses, and on foot to trace the Marsyangdi River to the circuit's first man-made highlight – the suspension bridge in Khudi – and your first glimpses of the majestic Manaslu range. The next six or seven days are spent following the Marsyangdi River to the very Tibetan-looking town of Manang with its sea of prayer flags, a world apart at 11,545 ft/3,519 m in its broad valley to the north of the Annapurna range with stunning views across the valley to the Annapurna Himal's northern wall.

Manang has a population of around 6,000, as well as a busy medical centre specialising in the treatment of altitude sickness, a common complaint of trekkers who really need to spend a day here to acclimatise before beginning the climb to Thorong La Pass on the edge of the Tibetan Plateau. At 17,769 ft/5,416 m it is the world's highest mountain pass, the circuit's highest point, and a crossing that should never be underestimated, even in good conditions. You can see four of the ten highest summits in the world from here, their ridges and flanks blanketed in a mix of sunlight and shadows beneath spindrifts of snow, blown by the wind into curling patterns above their towering peaks.

Once over the pass your goal is Muktinath (12,300 ft/3,750 m), a sacred place for Hindus and Buddhists, from which you descend into the upper reaches of the immense Kali Gandaki gorge, the world's deepest if you measure it against the summit of neighbouring Annapurna I (26,545 ft/8,091 m). On the way you pass Kagbeni, a charming alleyway-filled village resonant of a European alpine town, and Jomsom on the banks of the Kali Gandaki River with the majestic peaks of Dhaulagiri and Nilgiri brooding away in the background. The trail from Jomsom to Pokhara is a blessing to experience, following the Kali Gandaki River between Annapurna and Dhaulagiri with views over 8 of the world's 20 highest peaks along the way. The rock-encrusted trail, like everywhere on this trek, is easy to navigate and well defined, taking you down from barren high plateau-like landscapes into forests of rhododendrons, past poinsettia bushes and under spectacular rocky cliffs, and over some seriously long rope bridges, the river roaring below you all the while.

Plenty of excellent lodges line the route, and the hot springs at Tatopani will be a welcome relief to anyone with tired limbs – and that will be everyone – as they immerse themselves in its thermal waters. From Tatopani you continue on through Ghorepani to Ghorepani Pass, where you need to depart from the trail and, after a good night's sleep, begin the one-hour climb to Poon Hill where one of the greatest panoramas anywhere in the world awaits you – Dhalagiri (26,794 ft/8,167 m); Tukuche (22,802 ft/6,950 m); Nilgiri (22,998 ft/7,010 m); Annapurna I (26,545 ft/8,091 m) and more. Once on Poon Hill you have various optional trails available to you, but to continue on the main Annapurna Circuit you should descend back along the trail you just took and then continue on to Beni, where you can catch a bus back to Pokhara (even though the road now extends all the way to Jomsom – but this fact can, and should, be ignored).

Road building over the years, while greatly improving the lives of the local people, has gradually eroded the trail's reputation as the world's greatest walk. Of the 23 days that all originally had to be hoofed, now only a few days remain where walking trails are the only option. Nevertheless one can always walk if one wants to, roads or no roads, and there are still plenty of people like myself out there who prefer to call this magnificent walk by its grand old nickname: The Perfect Circle.

Photo: travelwaysoflife

3. PENNINE WAY NATIONAL TRAIL
England /Scotland

Distance: 431 km
Grade: Strenuous
Time: 14–21 days

It's a cliché to call the Pennine Way the 'backbone of England', but it's true – a 431-km 'long green trail' that runs from the town of Edale in the Peak District north via the Yorkshire Dales and the Tyne Valley, Hadrian's Wall and the Cheviot Hills to the Scottish border at Kirk Yetholm. It was Britain's first national trail, and remains its most loved. Forty thousand feet of accumulated elevation gain await you if you hike it right through, yet despite its deserved reputation for being the toughest of Britain's long distance walks its mostly gentle gradients are easier on the joints than ascending on shorter, steeper slogs. Here your biggest concern is and always will be the weather. A series of fine days and you'll have an adventurous, pleasant three weeks. If the weather turns nasty – and this is the high moors so you bet it will – this Jekyll and Hyde trail can suddenly begin to loom as a genuine obstacle, though not as a test of physical strength. On the Pennine Way the challenges are far more subtle – challenges born of logistics, of mental toughness. And loneliness.

Like most things in life worth having, the Pennine Way wasn't just dumped in our laps. It had to be fought for. In 1935 Tom Stephenson was a journalist working as the 'rural correspondent' for the *Daily Herald* newspaper when a letter arrived on his desk written by two American women enquiring whether there might be a long distance trail anywhere in the UK similar to America's Appalachian Trail that they might be able to walk during an upcoming holiday. Stephenson was all too familiar with the answer. In the 1930s much of northern England remained in private hands, and the famous mass trespass at Kinder Scout in Derbyshire in 1932 – when over 400 men and women protested against the lack of access to open country owned by landed gentry – became one of the most successful acts of civil disobedience in British history. 'Our request, or demand', said the group's spokesman Benny Rothman, 'for access to all peaks and uncultivated moorland is nothing unreasonable'.

Nothing unreasonable indeed. Three weeks later, 10,000 ramblers held a rally in Castleton demanding the same rights that put five of the Kinder Scout protesters into prison, and in the years that followed walkers' continual lobbying and cajoling of MPs eventually paved the way for the establishment of a network of national parks and long distance trails that would forever open up Britain's woodlands, moorlands, dales and chalk downs to its people. It also had to be waited for. The Pennine Way wouldn't open in its entirety until April of 1962, but when it did it was Tom Stephenson, then 72 years of age, who wrote its first guide book. And the route that was chosen would follow – with remarkably few deviations – the path Stephenson himself had mapped.

It begins in the land of the 'Dark Peaks' not far from Kinder Scout, the high, wild, bleak north of the Peak District, a land of Millstone Grit-covered limestone with a soil that every winter is saturated with water, a moorland plateau full of sphagnum bogs and the blackest of black peat. Coming off the plateau you descend past reservoirs with fabulous views over Manchester down into the Calder Valley and its

Photo: Kreuzschnabel

woodland river valleys before climbing again, this time over the Haworth moors of West Yorkshire. This is Bronte country. Stop to visit the family vault in Haworth and lament the fact that within eight brief years after the publication in 1847 of *Jane Eyre*, *Agnes Grey* and *Wuthering Heights*, all of their three authors – sisters Charlotte, Anne and Emily – were dead.

You now head into North Yorkshire into the rolling farmlands of the Aire Gap, a pass carved by Ice Age glaciers between the Craven Fault and the Yorkshire Dales' limestone uplands, a corridor between Yorkshire and Lancashire. Some serious hills now lie ahead of you – Fountains Fell and Pen-y-Ghent, before ancient droving roads take you to Hawes and over Great Shunner Fell to the delights of Swaledale, arguably Yorkshire's most beautiful dale. A further ascent takes you to the 17th-century Tan Hill Inn, at 1,732 ft England's highest pub with its gorgeous stone-flagged floors and roaring fireplace. The moors continue to the Stainmore Gap and on to Teesdale, one of England's most picturesque valleys, before the emptiness of Stainmore Common takes you from east to west across the watershed of the Pennines into the Eden Valley, followed by a long day's walk over the peaks of the Pennines to Alston and the Maiden Way, a 20-mile-long Roman road that later reverted to a drover's trail.

After paralleling Hadrian's Wall for some 11 miles the trail leaves the Pennines behind as it enters Northumberland Forest Park, a section that brings another day of solitude on the moors until you reach Byrness at the foot of the Cheviot Hills. You now have the final stage all before you, and it is not for the faint-of-heart – a bleak, unpopulated, inhospitable, 26.5-mile stretch at a minimum through the Cheviot Hills, including a series of summit-col-summit-col switchbacks of Beefstand Hill, high in the midst of an endless sea of rolling moorlands. If you're running out of daylight by the time you reach Border Ridge your best option if you've a tent is to camp wild at Davidson's Linn. Better still to depart Byrness before first light to allow enough time to enjoy your approach to Kirk Yetholm and The Border Hotel, the Pennine Way's official terminus.

You'll need to think about logistics. Head south to north so the rain and wind will mostly be at your back. Allow three weeks, not two, or you'll be rushing it, and that's not why you're here. Warm, waterproof clothing and decent walking boots are a must, as are a compass and a 1:25,000 scale map. And even though many of the very worst sections of mud and bogs are now paved, prepare for mud and bogs nonetheless so you'll be able to trudge through whatever this trail can throw at you and not let conditions detract from the beauty and majesty of the wild countryside that surrounds you.

2. APPALACHIAN TRAIL
Georgia to Maine, USA

Distance: 3,476 km
Grade: Easy to Strenuous
Time: 5–7 months

They call it the 'long, green tunnel', a never-ending canopy of green that envelops you, disorientates you, that even can prevent you from seeing where you are. The Appalachian Trail (AT), given its shape by half a billion years of geology, begins – or ends, as most prefer to hike it south to north – at Springer Mountain in Georgia and ends almost 3,500 km northeast at Mount Katahdin in the New England state of Maine. It is one of the celebrated 'Triple Crowns' of American long distance hikes, along with the Pacific Crest Trail and the Continental Divide Trail. And it is by far the most revered. Millions walk at least a section of it every year, and each year around 2,000 people set out to conquer it in a 'thru-hike'. Nine out of ten don't make it.

The trail was first born in the mind of Benton MacKaye, the great American forester and conservationist who first thought of it, he said, while sitting in a tree on Vermont's Stratton Mountain. MacKaye had long dreamt of creating a practical refuge for America's urban populations, and was inspired by the success of Vermont's Long Trail, built over 20 years from 1910 to 1930 by Vermont's Green Mountain Club. MacKaye then wrote a paper on the proposed new trail in the October 1921 issue of the *Journal of the American Institute of Architects*. His idea was quick to evolve, and it has since become America's most-trodden footpath.

Springer Mountain, an area of Georgia that has never been forested because of its boulder-strewn soil, is, in many ways, an ideal place for the trail to officially begin. But it can be a heartbreaking start for the novice who will likely sign in at the visitor centre at Amicalola Falls – only to be told the official Springer Mountain starting point is almost 13 km away on a gradual ascent. One Appalachian myth says you can arrive here with nothing on your back, and by the time you've walked your first few kilometres you will have managed to fully equip yourself with everything you need by just picking through all the abandoned gear you'll be stepping over. Well, it's not quite that bad ...

The Appalachian Trail was completed in 1937. It passes through fourteen states, has an accumulated gain/loss of an astonishing 464,500 ft (there are some flat areas on the trail, but they are few and far between), receives 3 million visitors a year, and follows, as the name suggests, the Appalachian Mountains, a system of mountains that includes their surrounding hills and a region of dissected plateau that runs from the Canadian province/island of Newfoundland southwest all the way to Central Alabama. It is filled with a bounty of deciduous trees: yellow buckeye, sugar maple, American beech, white ash, yellow birch, red maple and hickory, with an understorey of flowering dogwoods, witch-hazel and bloodroot. There's a purpose-built shelter – the so-called 'lean-tos' – every eight miles on average, which means it's feasible to hike the AT without carrying a tent. The shelters are free, too, and the fact you don't require a tent means you're carrying less weight, a blessing on a trail that is often heavily rock-strewn. Which brings to mind another thru-hiker joke: that if you happen to lose the trail, don't despair. Just look for the rocks and you'll be fine.

And it is a 'trail of statistics', unlike any other. In any given year over 6,000 volunteers from more than 30 Appalachian Trail clubs will give up over 200,000 hours repairing trails and maintaining shelters; if you're soaking wet with a 32-lb pack you'll burn 450 calories in an hour; toilets cannot be dug closer than 200 ft from the trail and must be at least six inches deep; it'll take you 285,700 steps to travel 125 miles; and the trail crosses a road on average every four miles.

It's impossible to provide a detailed route description for a trail this long. It scales the summit of Georgia's Blood Mountain (4,461 ft), passes through the Great Smoky Mountains of North Carolina and Tennessee, and traverses the West Virginia/Virginia border before arriving at its half-way point at historic Harper's Ferry. It runs below the ridgeline of Maryland's South Mountain, a northern extension of the Blue Ridge range, threads the needle through the Delaware Water Gap on the Pennsylvania/

Photo: Nicholas A. Tonelli

New Jersey border, and crosses New York's Hudson River. In Connecticut it follows the ridges above the Housatonic River, passes through Massachusetts' Berkshire County and the Green Mountains of Vermont, and climbs 17 of New Hampshire's 48 4,000-footers. Finally, it enters Maine, fording dozens of icy rivers and streams, goes headlong through Maine's 'Hundred-Mile Wilderness' – the trail's wildest traverse – and ends at Mount Katahdin in Baxter State Park.

But what makes this trail so extraordinary isn't the pathway or the views – it is the people you meet along the way. The AT teaches you how to be vulnerable, how to ask for assistance from strangers when you need it, and to share experiences with people you do not know. Coming here in winter will draw you away from all the things you consider are comfortable. Sections might only be completed thanks to the intervention and grace of strangers. You'll likely hitchhike at some point to get from the trail to a town in order to buy supplies. 'Hostel owners' are the trail's angels, sharing their homes with hikers and asking for little in return.

There are little vignettes along the AT that you'll never forget. The 'rollercoaster' is a 14.5-mile section in Virginia with a highly compacted series of 'ups and downs' over about eleven adjacent hills for a total elevation gain of 5,000 ft. The Webster Cliff Trail in New Hampshire will sap your energy as you climb over two strenuous miles for the privilege of standing atop a line of forbidding cliffs that look more like fortress walls, overlooking the hamlet of Crawford Notch. And then there's arguably the trail's finest ridge walk – 14 miles along Tennessee's remote Iron Mountain on narrow, graded paths and old logging roads.

But whether it's the wilderness you conquer, the tribulations you endure, or the angels you meet along the way with their all-you-can-eat dinners, the Appalachian Trail has the capacity to change lives. It is so much more than just a walk in the woods. To use it is to connect with nature, and with each other.

It is a journey.

1. MOUNT KAILASH
China (Tibet)

Distance: 52 km
Grade: Strenuous
Time: 3 days

It is an irony born of isolation: the world's most revered holy place is also the least visited. Mount Kailash (22,028 ft) in western Tibet was being venerated long before the arrival of Hinduism. It is Mount Miri, the *Axis Mundi* – the axis upon which the world turns – the world's epicentre, our 'navel', the birthplace of our planet. For Hindus it is the realm of Lord Shiva, the destroyer of ignorance who lives there in eternal meditation. For the Jains it is Meru Parvat, where the first Jain attained Nirvana. The founder of the Bon religion, a Tibetan sect with similarities to Tibetan Buddhism, also dwells on Kailash, and for Tantric Buddhists it is the home of Demchok, the embodiment of supreme bliss.

Religious pilgrims come here in their thousands every year to walk once around the mountain, a holy ritual called the *kora* which, it is believed, will bring good fortune, if not salvation. Hikers and adventurers come here from around the world, drawn in part by the mountain's mysticism and rich

Photo: Ondrej Žváček

mythology but also by the tapestry of challenges the 52-km walk around its base represents, involving uneven terrain, multiple crossings of difficult mountain passes, including the 5,669-m-high Dolma La Pass, and the risk of altitude sickness due to the average 5,000-m-plus elevation of the trail that encircles this pyramidal mountain. Its four striated faces give it a beauty and an overwhelming presence that sets it apart from many higher though far more 'common' Himalayan peaks.

Nowadays you are not permitted to climb Kailash, and it is said that those who have gone to the summit in the past never returned. In 1985 the great Italian mountaineer Reinhold Messner was given permission to climb it but refused, saying that to climb Kailash would be like trampling on people's souls.

Pilgrims usually aim to circumnavigate Kailash in a day, while some Tibetans may continue to circle the mountain and might make as many as 108 circuits. The walk, which is best done between May and October, requires a considerable commitment of time and resources, and just getting there is something of an achievement. The most popular approach has always been from the Tibetan capital of Lhasa, from which there is both a northern and a southern route that, with the aid of a 4WD, will get you to the walk's starting point – the nondescript 'seasonal' village of Darchen, which will be full of tents at pilgrimage time. Since June 2015, however, a new route using buses from the town of Nathula in Sikkim has been opened by the Chinese government, an approach which will slash 'commuting' time to Kailash to just two-and-a-half days.

Most set out in a clockwise direction from Darchen (Buddhist and Hindu pilgrims and the majority of hikers walk in a clockwise direction, while adherents of the Bon faith walk it counter-clockwise), and the trail itself is of course somewhat predictable and well worn, the choices of where to spend each night are fairly straightforward. Day 1 will see you set out from Darchen and spend the night at Drirapuk Gompa; Day 2 will have you depart Drirapuk Gompa for Zutrulpuk Gompa; and on Day 3 you will head out of Zutrulpuk Gompa back to Darchen. It may read as if it's straightforward, but this circuit is a challenge, a true test of mind, body and spirit.

Heading out from Darchen into the unending barrenness before you, the landscape soon broadens to provide enticing views over fertile green valleys, deep blue lakes and perennially snow-capped peaks. A cairn at 4,730 m will give you your first look at Kailash's southern face, and from there you follow the Lha-chu Valley (you can walk along either bank of the Lha-chu River) all the way to Drirapuk. The next day if you're feeling particularly energetic and get up early enough you can make the two-hour return trek to Kangkyam Glacier on the mountain's north face; otherwise just steel yourself for the ascent to Dolma La Pass, the circuit's high point, before making the hour-long 400-m descent to the green embankments of the Lha-chu Valley and a three-hour hike to some lovely flat grassy fields – or push on another hour and you'll reach the relative comfort of Zutrulpuk Gompa's simple guesthouse. From Zutrulpuk the trail parallels the river and leads into the Barkha Valley and along a dirt road that will take you back to your starting point at Darchen.

Before you arrive to begin your Tibetan adventure, a little time spent researching the circuit from a pilgrim's point of view will greatly enhance your experience of what many people consider the world's greatest walk. Virtually all of the surrounding peaks, rocky promontories and various rock outgrowths have their own religious significance, their own stories to tell. There are five monasteries around Kailash: Nyari, Drirapuk, Songchu, Gyangzha and Thailong, and a visit should be made to them all, as each has its own very distinct hoard of legendary stories to share. All might be in various stages of decay, but each is able and very happy to offer accommodation if you want to transform your three-day circuit into something a little longer.

It's also well worth looking a little further afield now that you've made all the effort just to get here and make a visit (permits required from the Cultural Relics Bureau in Lhasa) to Tibet's very own hidden 'Shangri-La' – the ancient kingdom of Guge in the Garuda Valley – home to the 'lost' cities of Toling and Tsaparang with their astonishing array of 10th- and 11th-century monastic ruins, fortifications, temples and palaces. Tsaparang still contains Tibet's greatest concentration of Buddhist art.

You'll want to keep your eye out for wildlife too because although the Tibetan Plateau might be a desert, it is hardly devoid of life. Bar-headed geese and ducks can be found on Kailash's surrounding lakes, and Siberian cranes migrate through here on their way south to Nepal. There are mountain deer, antelope, and of course the ubiquitous yak (mostly domesticated, though wild yaks can be seen roaming the region's remote valleys). There are also domesticated sheep and goats, and the skittish, donkey-like *khyangs*, large reddish-brown wild asses.

When you walk around Kailash you won't be alone. You'll be sharing the trail with many pilgrims, some of whom have been preparing for years to come here. They potentially will become as integral a part of your Mount Kailash circuit as the mountain itself, and you shouldn't miss an opportunity to share with them your experiences and to learn what you can of their own journeys. Like many of the other walks in this book, this trail is as much about what you can learn, as what you can see.

NOTES

NOTES

NOTES

NOTES

NOTES

NOTES

Also available

ISBN: 9781785780264 (paperback) / 9781785780271 (ebook)

IN ASSOCIATION WITH
TIMPSON

Also available

PETER
PUGH

MOST INFLUENTIAL
BRITONS
OF THE LAST 100 YEARS

ISBN: 9781785780349 (paperback) / 9781785780356 (ebook)

IN ASSOCIATION WITH
TIMPSON

Also available

the 50

ANTHONY LAMBERT

GREATEST TRAIN JOURNEYS OF THE WORLD

ISBN: 9781785780653 (paperback) / 97817857880660 (ebook)